A PHOTOGRAPHIC MEMORY | George S. Hutton

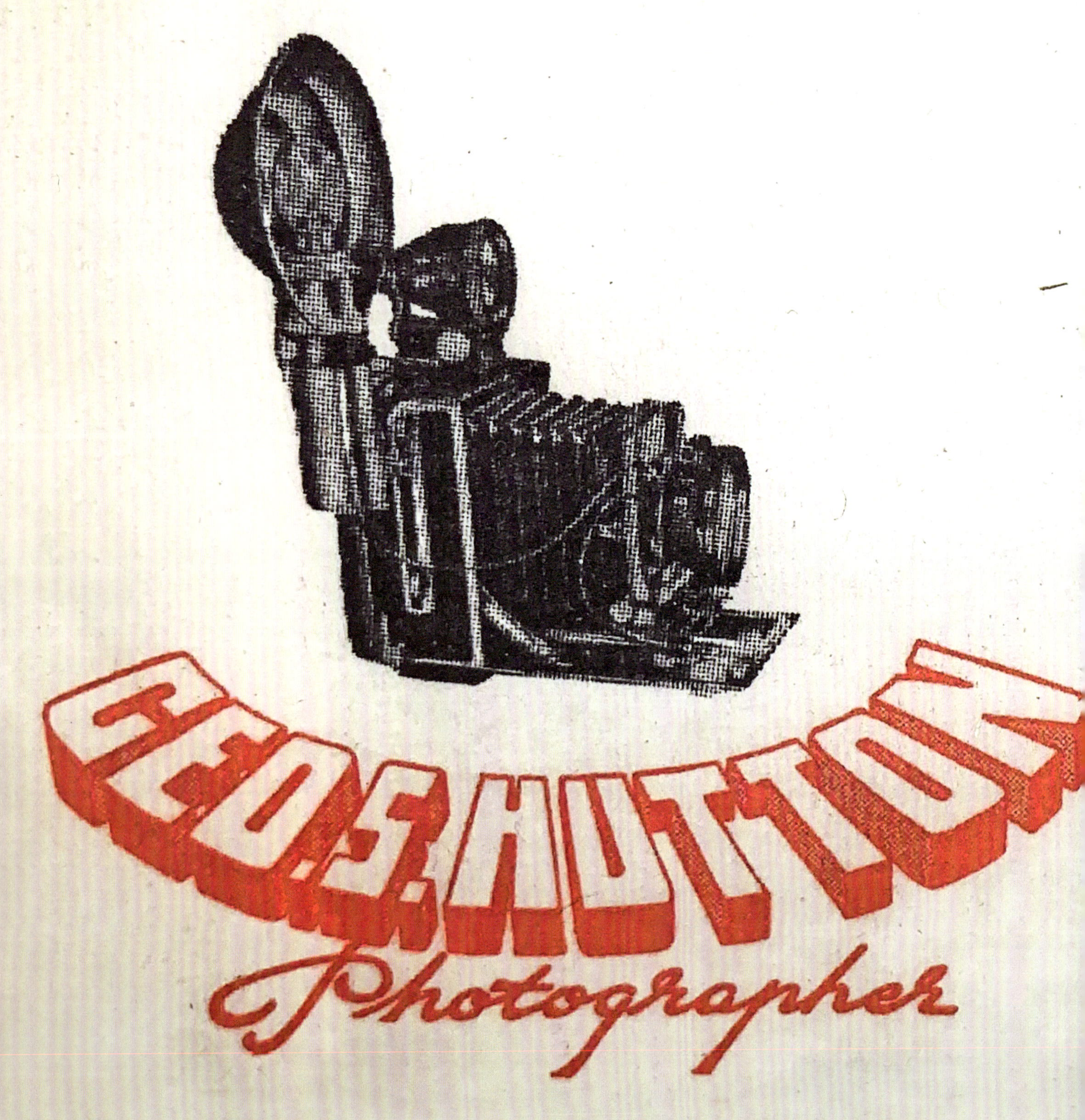
GEO. S. HUTTON
Photographer

A PHOTOGRAPHIC MEMORY

George S. Hutton's Port Adelaide and surrounds, 1924 to 1984

| Erina S. Hutton |

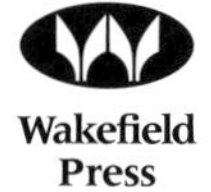

Wakefield Press

DEDICATION

To George, Audrey and the Hutton family: past, present and future.

ACKNOWLEDGEMENTS

Thanks to the History Trust of South Australia for helping to make possible the sharing of George's story and his iconic images.

To Peter and Dominic Newnham for technical assistance, support and endless patience.

To Lise Windsor for a shared love of history and constant encouragement.

To Brian Samuels for his encyclopaedic knowledge of the Port and surrounds.

To Clive, Deane and Rex Hutton, Jess Stapledon, June Harman and Ron Blum, for sharing their memories.

To Wakefield Press for publishing George's photographs for all to enjoy.

And to Atkins Photo Lab for developing and printing vintage high-quality professional images.

Note: not all of the negatives and prints discovered in the Hutton archives were annotated with dates, so an approximation is used where possible.

WAKEFIELD PRESS

16 Rose Street
Mile End
South Australia 5031
www.wakefieldpress.com.au

First published 2019
Reprinted 2020, 2021

Designed by Liz Nicholson, Wakefield Press
Printing and quality control in China by Tingleman P/L

ISBN 978 1 74305 669 1

A catalogue record for this book is available from the National Library of Australia

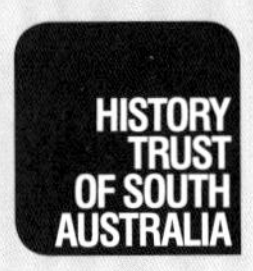

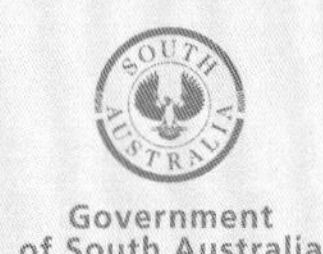

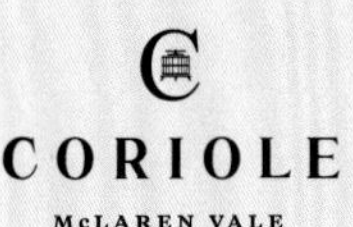

CONTENTS

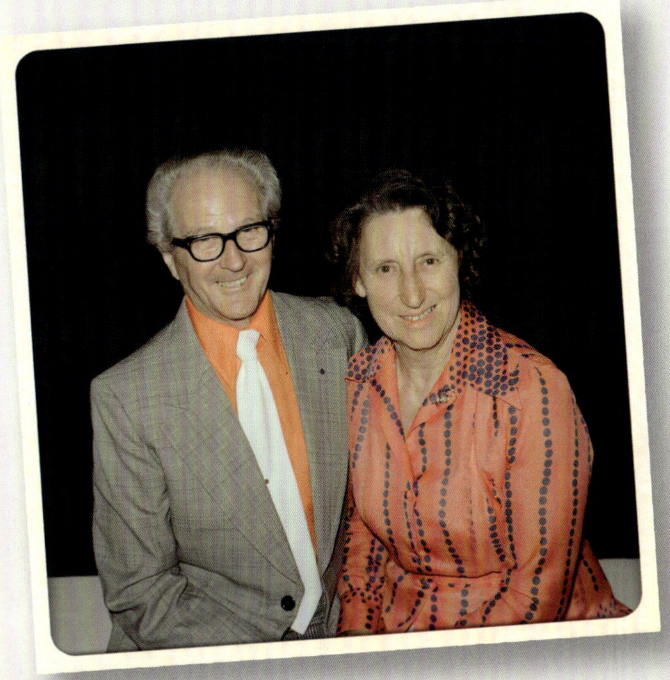

Above: George and Audrey, 1975

This book will appeal to anyone with long-standing connections to the Port Adelaide district, but also offers insights into everyday life that have broader appeal to South Australians generally.

There have been many photographic studios in the Port district through the years and their work has captured much of the area's rich history. Thanks to his daughter Erina, George Hutton's is the first to have a book devoted to it, and his output well warrants it.

George's work was not confined to the studio. It included work for many local schools and businesses and, as a long-term local resident, much photographing of local events and street scenes.

Years after sitting before him for annual school class photos, I served with George on the Port Adelaide Historical Society's Committee and discovered that he was a photographer with a photographic memory. His ability to put names to the faces in his photos was extraordinary.

Many images here will stir memories for South Australians everywhere. Some examples are:

- The SS *Karatta* that served on the Port Adelaide–Kingscote run, 1907–61.
- The Semaphore Town Hall – one of the early venues of the Ozone Picture Company (founded at Semaphore) – after its 1929 makeover into a fully-fledged Ozone Theatre. The Ozone chain grew to almost 30 cinemas before Hoyts Theatres Ltd bought into the business in 1951.
- A special steam train on the Glanville–Semaphore line in 1978, the year the main street railway was closed after a century of service.

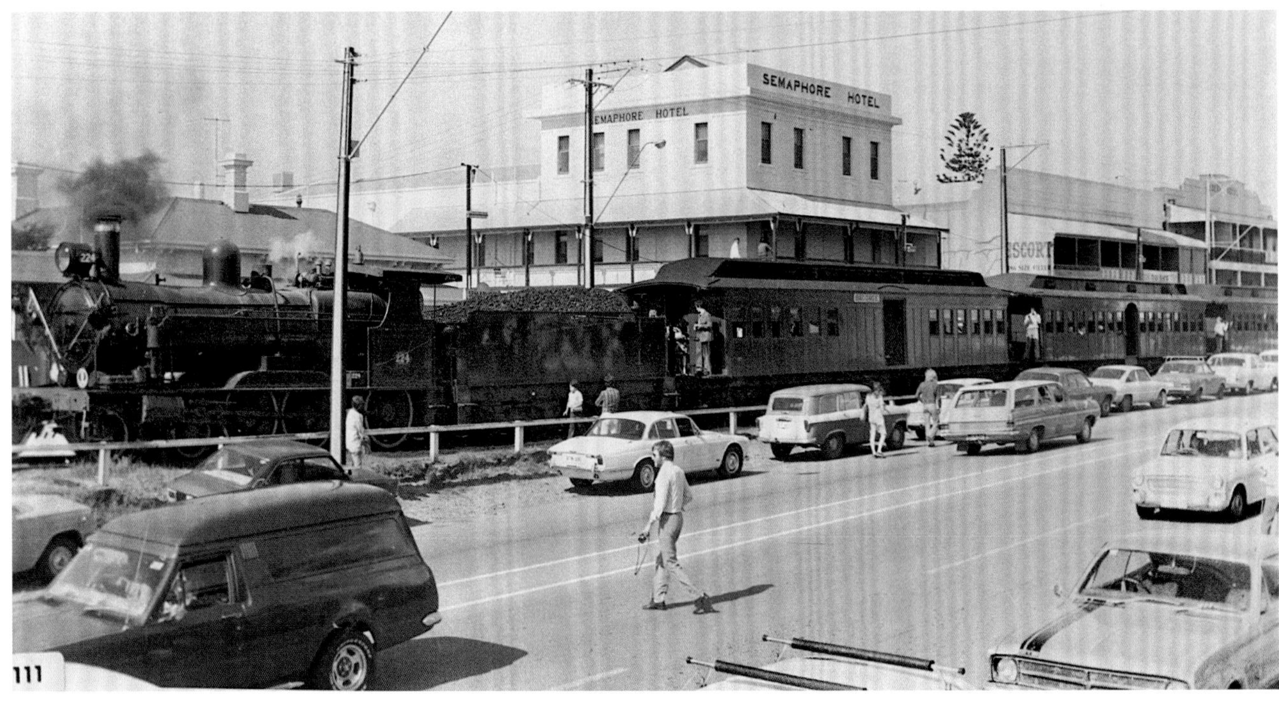

- The bandstands on the foreshore at Largs and Semaphore, both hubs of seaside entertainment.
- The Semaphore Bathing Pavilion and Palais (opened 1922; now the Palais Hotel), which included a kiosk, dance hall, roof garden and observation tower.

More generally, changing fashions in dress are captured on the beach, in street scenes, and in wedding photos ranging from the 1930s to the 1980s.

Many of the photos are previously unpublished and are being made easily accessible here for the first time. However, as a long-standing enthusiast of South Australian history, I know that many historically significant photos and negatives are still being discarded across the state.

If the images in this book speak to you, please consider spreading the word to families and friends that it's highly desirable to offer state or local libraries, museums and historical groups a chance to peruse such collections for items warranting preservation in perpetuity.

Brian Samuels

Hon. Historian to the Port Adelaide Historical Society 1973–1994

Member, Professional Historians Association (SA) 1982–present

Opposite: A special steam train to Semaphore in 1978, the year the main street railway was closed after a century of service.

Below: Semaphore Road looking East, showing the town hall venue of the Ozone Theatre after it had reopened as the Semaphore Cinema, 1970s.

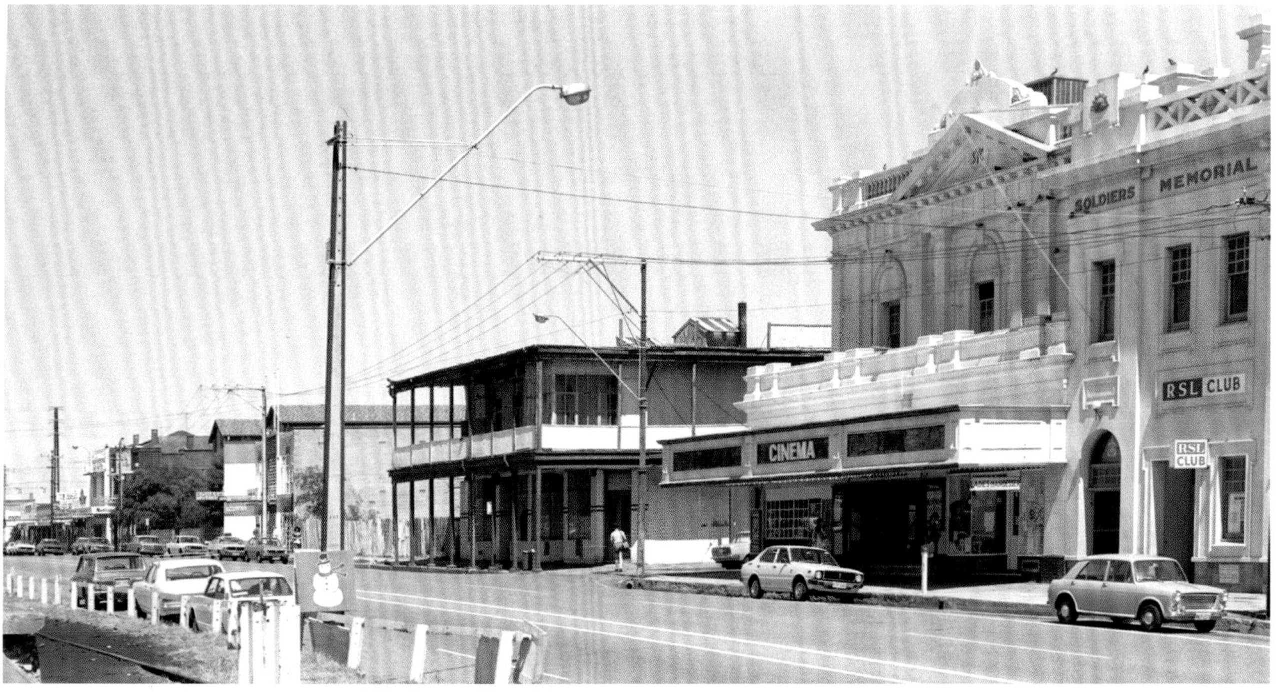

| PREFACE |

Growing up in a photographer's family meant that everything – whether it was pets, new cars, or outings – was photographed. Unlike today, however, the photographs did not appear instantly. A darkroom in the house guaranteed quick results if black-and-white film was being used, but it could take about a week for colour photographs to come back from the lab.

The excitement of going to the studio as a small child remains a vivid memory, especially when swanning about the dressing room with its glamorous, light-bulb encircled Hollywood mirror.

Dad worked from home from 1964, which enabled him to show me how to develop and print my own films. It was magical to see ghostly images appear.

More memories from the home studio in the mid-1960s include the gorgeously attired bridal parties filing into the front room, Dad diving under the tartan cloth of the big old camera, my mother Audrey meticulously arranging the groups so that everything looked absolutely perfect. Mum using the dining-room table for careful measurement and cropping of the wedding photographs. And her constant pounding of the old Royal typewriter, cranking out letters and invoices and making numerous phone-calls to take bookings or chase payment. Scenes like this gave me an insight into the long hours and stresses of the family business.

This book of images brings together a selection of Dad's extraordinary photographs in an attempt to preserve his legacy, and to reflect the experience of a young man struggling to build a photography business in Adelaide during the Depression. He was a self-taught photographer, an active church member, a Rotarian, devoted husband and a much-loved father and grandfather.

On the wall of his studio, Dad displayed a quote from an unknown source, titled 'I am Photography'. It perfectly sums up what George's work meant to him, his family and his community:

'I turn back the pages of the book of memory. I bring you thoughts of past years and old time friends. I keep forever green the happy hours of childhood. I dull the pangs of bereavement and blunt the edge of the Grim Reaper's Scythe . . . I am an Art – and yet a Business. I am Photography.'

Erina Hutton, 2019

Below: George and Erina, Exeter studio, 1957.
Opposite: Movie camera, 1940s.

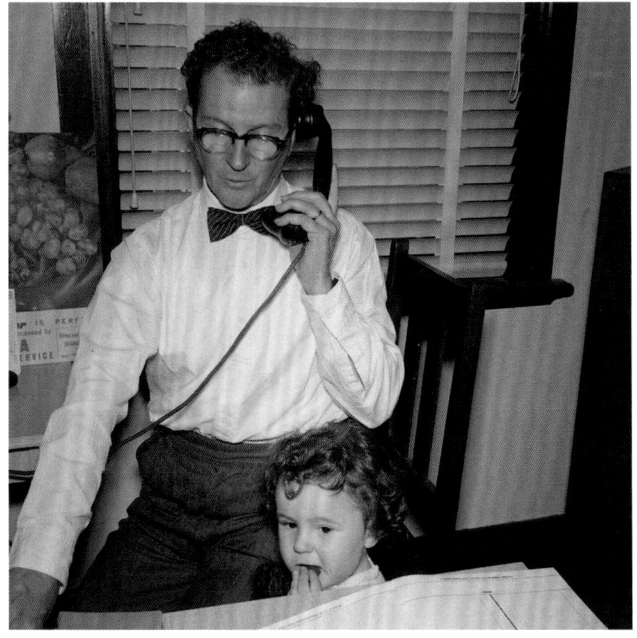

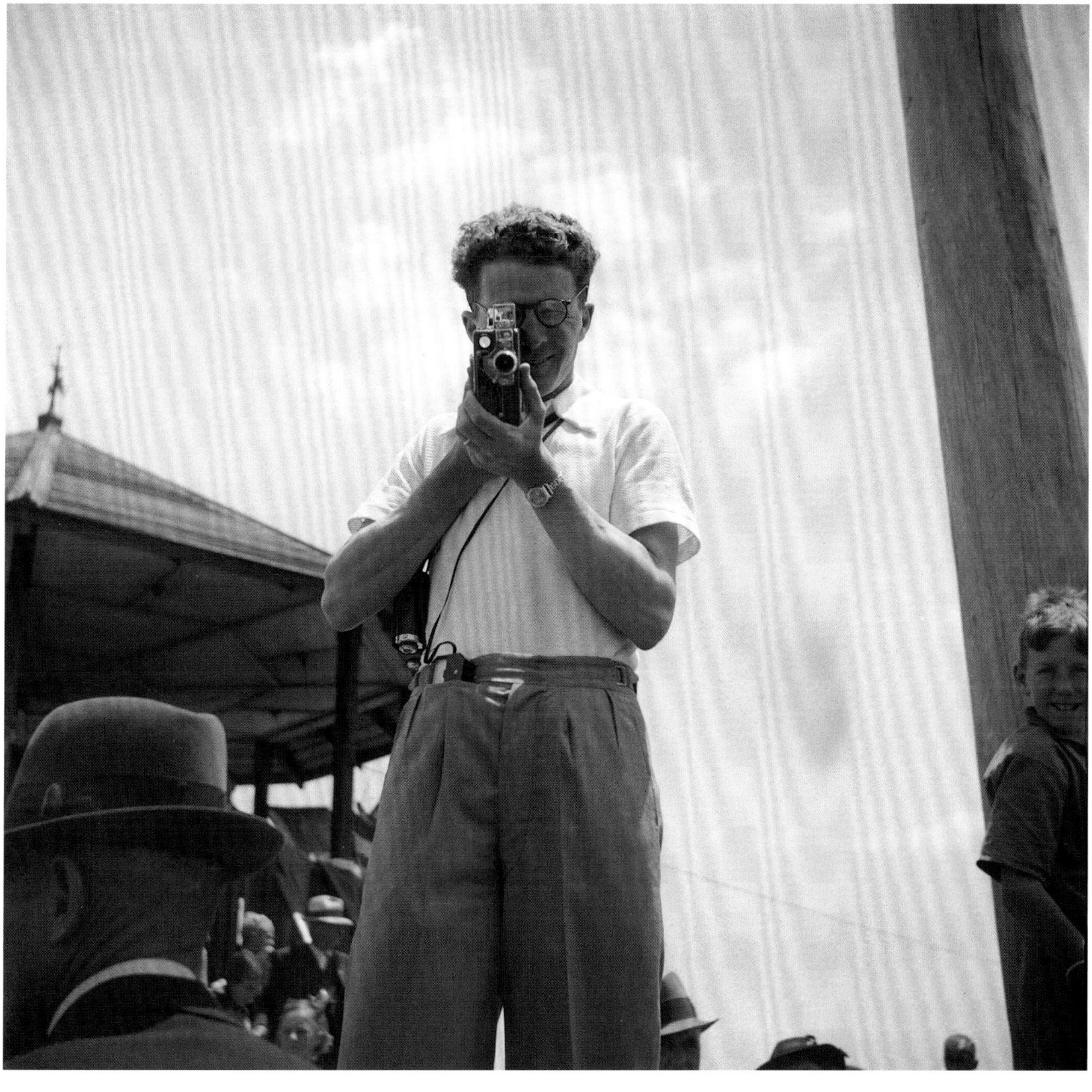

| INTRODUCTION |

Opposite: Knowles family; sisters Norma (top row), Laurel and Audrey, with mother Gertrude, 1942

George Stewart Hutton's link to photography began before he was born. His father, George Stewart Hutton senior, was so enamoured with the photograph of a young lady, Elizabeth McMillan, which he spotted in a photographer's window in late-1800s Glasgow, that he arranged to make her acquaintance. Successfully it seemed, as the couple had three children by 1909. George Stewart Junior (wee Georgie) was born in Glasgow, 1906 and the family migrated to South Australia with his sister Jean in 1912, to join elder brother Charlie and Uncle James and Aunt Catherine, who had set up house at Outer Harbor.

When George spoke to the Port Adelaide Historical Society about his career in 1982, he recalled that his interest in photography was sparked as a child: his father, a dental mechanic, made and used simple cameras.

The earliest of George's photographs date from around 1924, when he rekindled this interest at the age of 18. During bouts of unemployment and the Depression of the 1920s, he started thinking about making his hobby into a business.

George gained employment at The Glanville Pipe Works and Government Workshops, but work was spasmodic from 1927–1930. But he was not idle, and continued with his photography, taking portraits from the family home. In 1931, aged 25, he joined the Semaphore Baptist Church Dramatic Club, where he met a group of young people, including 16-year-old Audrey Knowles. From then on, he was a constant visitor to her family home in Dunn Street, Semaphore and he proposed to her in 1937. George wanted to establish his photography business before marrying and starting a family, so he took on as many weddings and portraits as he could, in order to buy better cameras and equipment.

George and Audrey married on 21 January 1939. George was now 32 and Audrey was 23. By this time, George had established a thriving portrait and wedding photography business from his first studio, on the corner of Woolnough Road in Exeter. World War II broke out in September of that year. Photography was a reserved occupation and George's work photographing young servicemen – and many hastily arranged wartime weddings – was important.

In her records, Audrey noted several wartime double weddings between 1940 and 1943. A double wedding was an economical way to organise a family celebration, with the costs of a reception and photographer shared between two couples. Audrey wrote in her diary one Easter Saturday: 'Had 13 bookings, it was a production line, with wedding parties climbing the narrow staircase to the studio, posing for the requisite bride, bride and groom, bride and bridesmaids, full wedding party and close-ups.'

In March 1940, the couple's first-born son, Clive, arrived. He was followed by Deane in 1941, then Rex in 1945. I was George and Audrey's only daughter: born nine years later, in 1954. Audrey efficiently managed the financial side of the photography business while rearing four children.

George had been interested in movie photography in the 1930s and continued throughout his life to film family events, though the materials were too expensive for him to work professionally with film. We have a copy of George's 1932 13-minute movie, *Alton Movie Club* (combining the names of H.W. Allen and George Hutton), which shows crowded Semaphore beach scenes, bathing beauty competitions and two short comic photoplays.

After World War II, Audrey and George wrote to photographers in the United Kingdom, exchanging news about their businesses and families. The correspondence continued for many years. George and Audrey met their correspondents and their families on their first overseas holiday in 1977, when George was 71.

As their correspondents grew, so did the idea of sending an annual photographic Christmas card, documenting George and Audrey's growing family. So in 1946, a pictorial card featuring a charming trio of young boys started a trend that lasted until 1975. Each year, Audrey sought new thematic inspiration and as

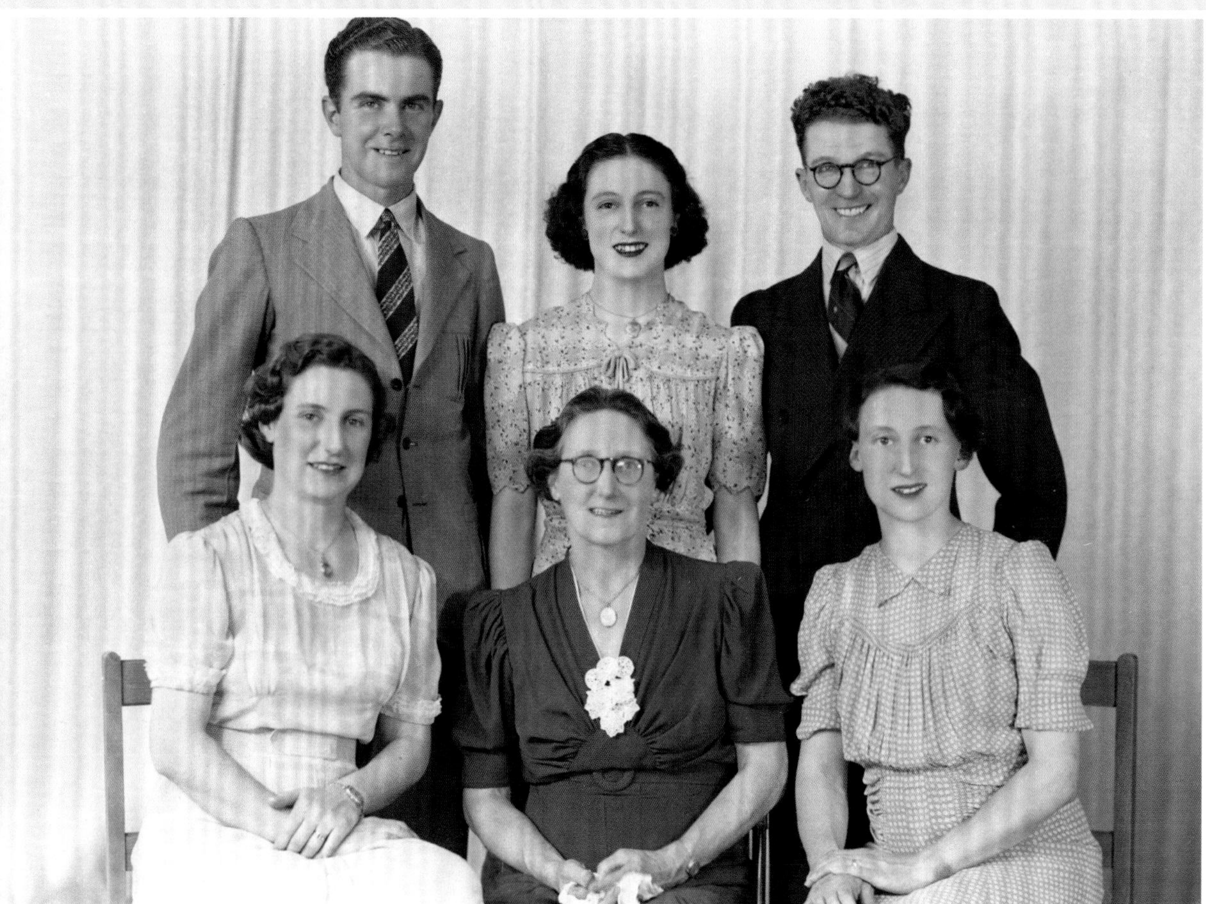

she devised more complex tableaux, their construction became more complex, too. In the days before Photoshop, this meant that numerous photographs were posed and taken, followed by literal cutting with scissors and pasting with glue – then further photographs, until the family were exhausted and the 'creative muse' was satisfied. Eldest sons Clive and Deane used their lettering skills to add seasonal greetings. Some years, a biblical text was incorporated to reflect the family's church background.

The business at the studio continued until 1965, but an increased demand for on-location work and a decline in hand-colouring eventually meant that a studio space was less necessary. George moved his studio to the Largs Bay family home, creating a darkroom and using the front room as his studio for another 18 years.

Commercial photography kept George busy and it was more financially rewarding than weddings and portraits. He photographed large buildings from foundations to completion, large-scale alterations to factories, oil installations for oil companies, and more. Between the 1930s and 1970s, various companies and organisations commissioned George to photograph their premises and staff. This was lucrative work: photographing a set amount, developing and printing within a few hours, and returning the finished product (sometimes the same day).

Dad worked occasionally into his late 70s, but at 77, after an illness-free, active life, he was diagnosed with cancer and died aged 78 on 7 October 1984.

Reverend John Roberts Thomson (a family friend) noted in his eulogy that 'for fifty years, to thousands of people in the community, George Hutton was the man with the camera who captured their images forever – in weddings, social events, school photographs, passports and family groups'.

George had the posthumous honour of having Hutton Place, near his original Exeter studio, named after him.

Erina Hutton, 2019

| SHIPS AND SHOPS |

In the course of his commercial photography, George captured many of the local businesses, ships and wharves, buildings and bridges in the Port Adelaide area, preserving them forever as they were. George's commercial work was more lucrative than weddings and portraits, and it kept him busy.

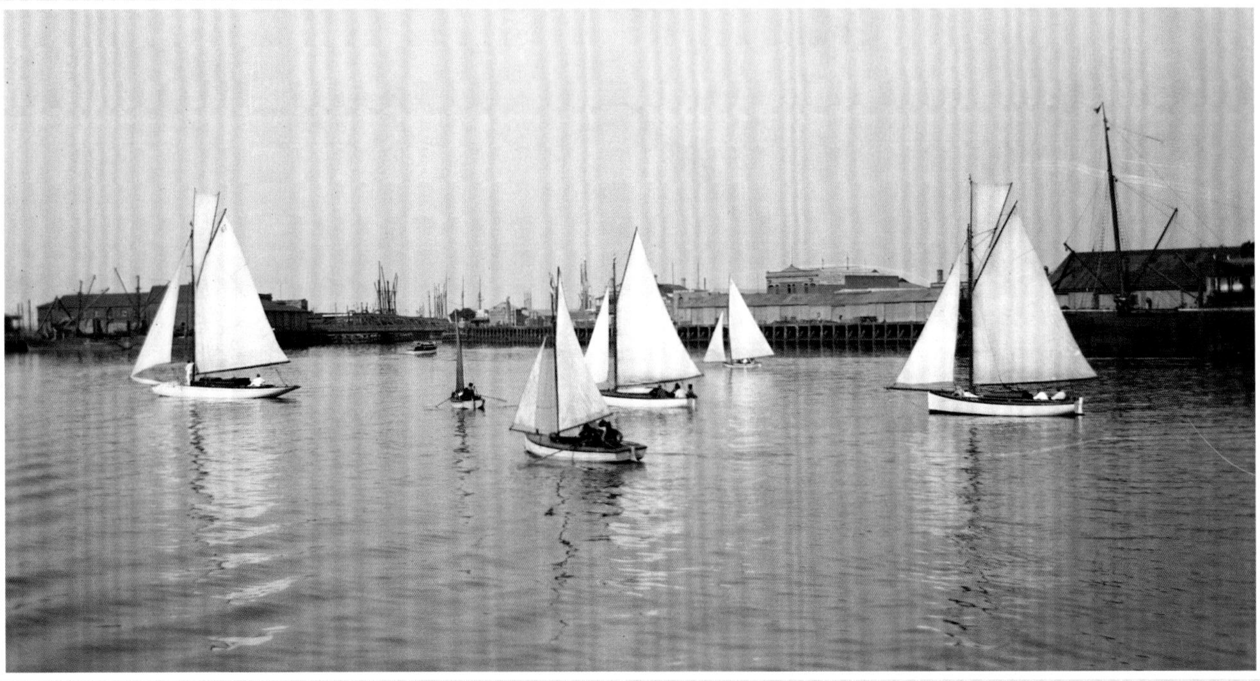

Above: Port River, yachts, 1920s.
Opposite: *Yalata*, Outer Harbor.

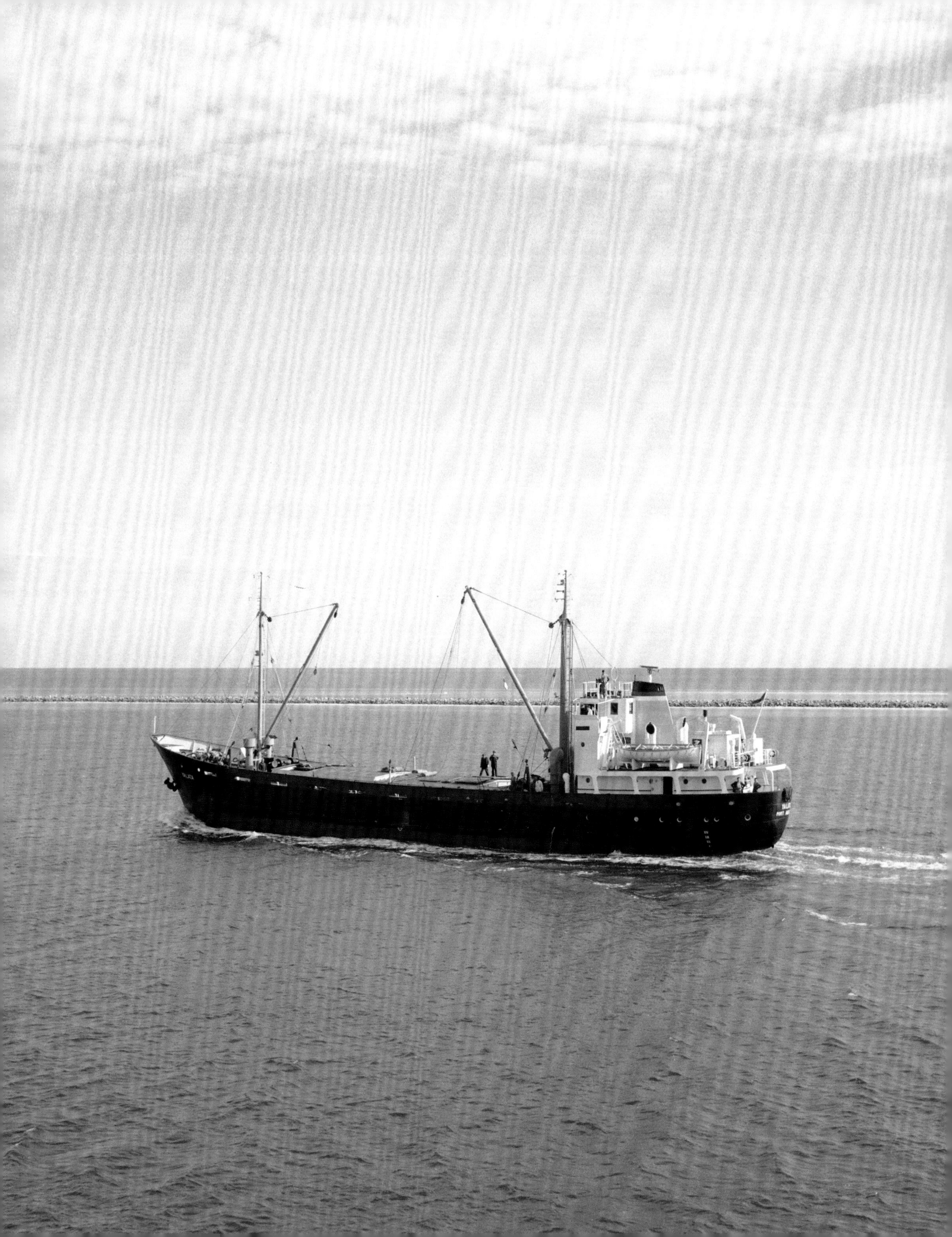

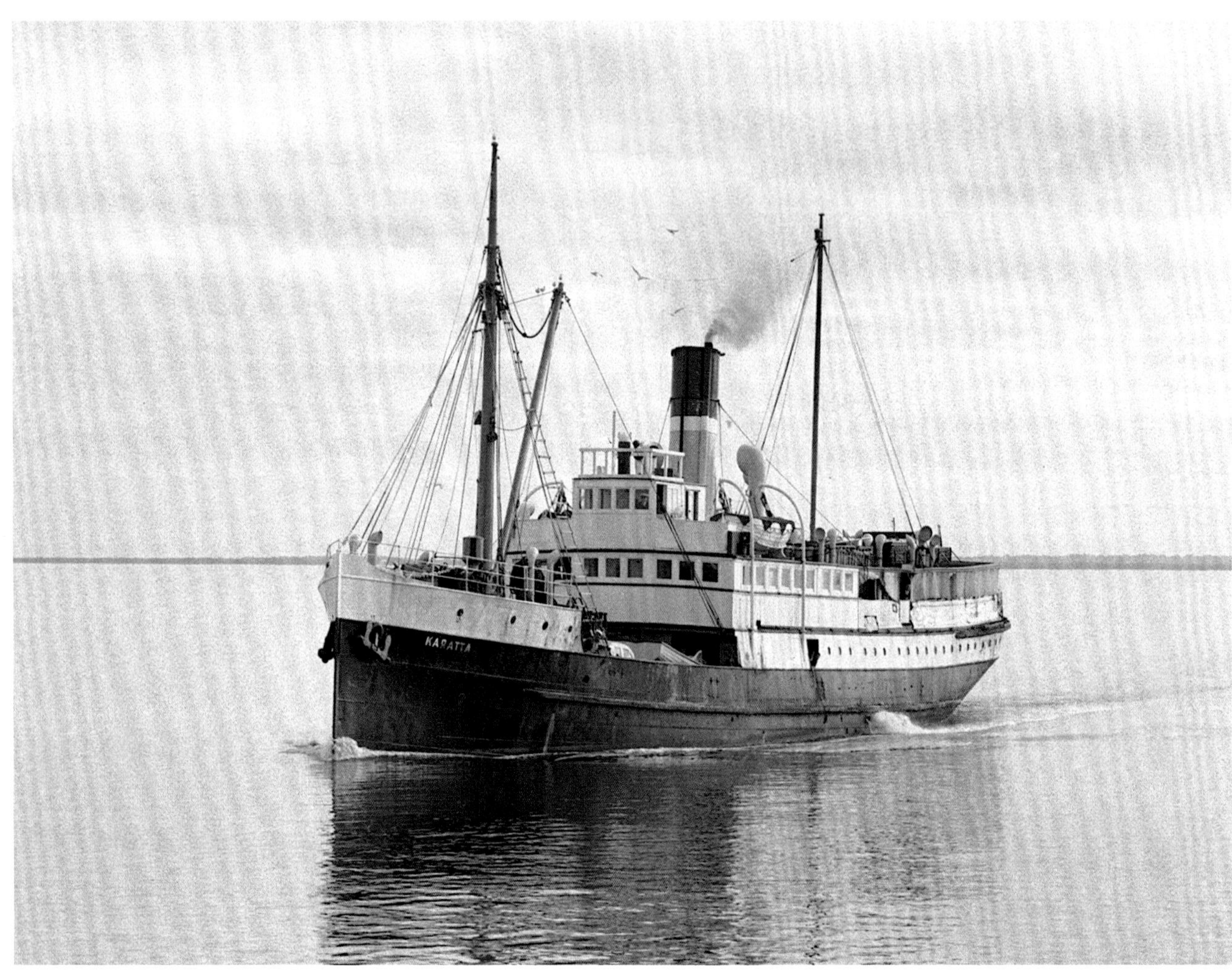

Above: *Karatta*, Outer Harbor, 1940s.

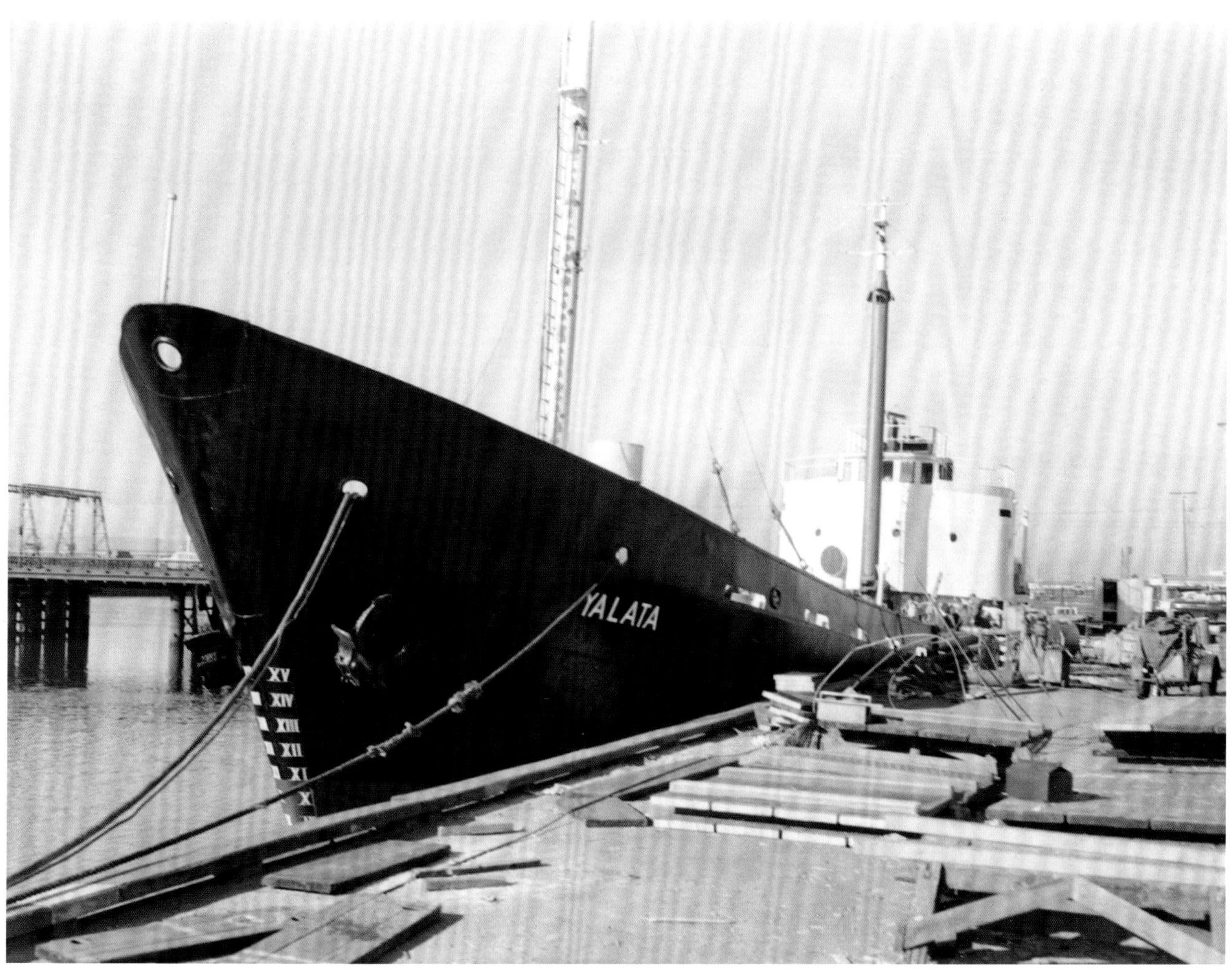

Above: *Yalata*, Port Adelaide, 1940s.

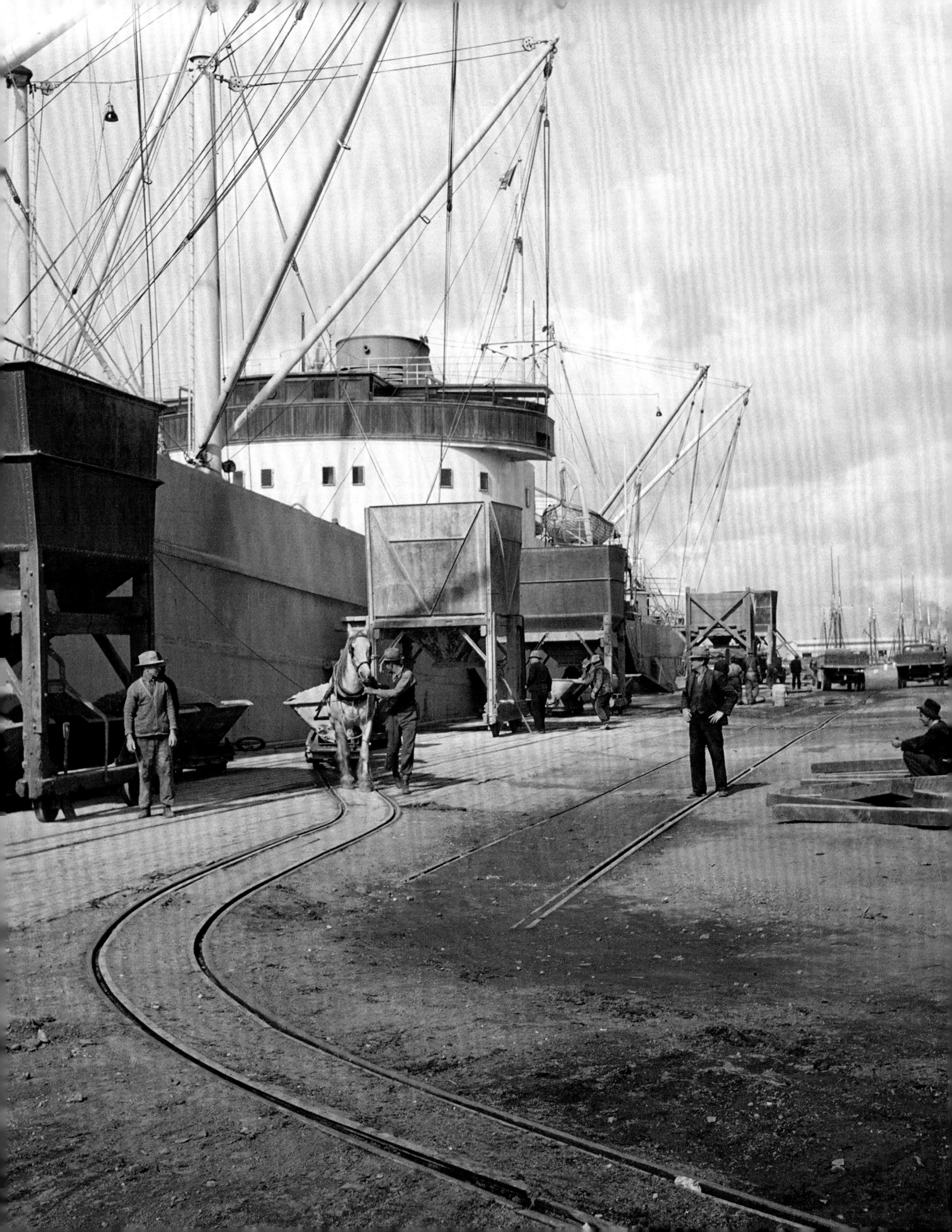

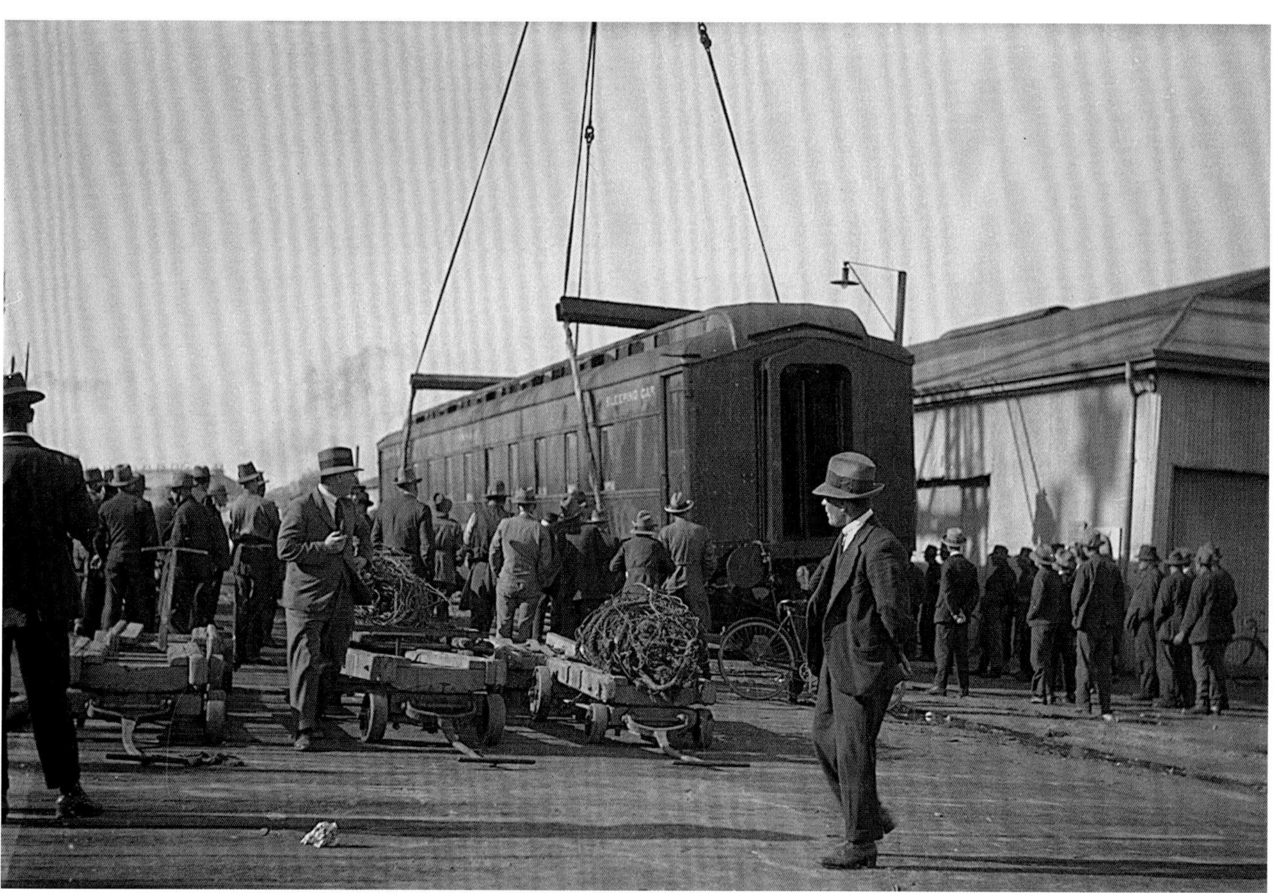

Above: Port Adelaide wharves, unloading a sleeping car, 1930s.
Opposite: Port Adelaide wharves, horsepower, 1930s.

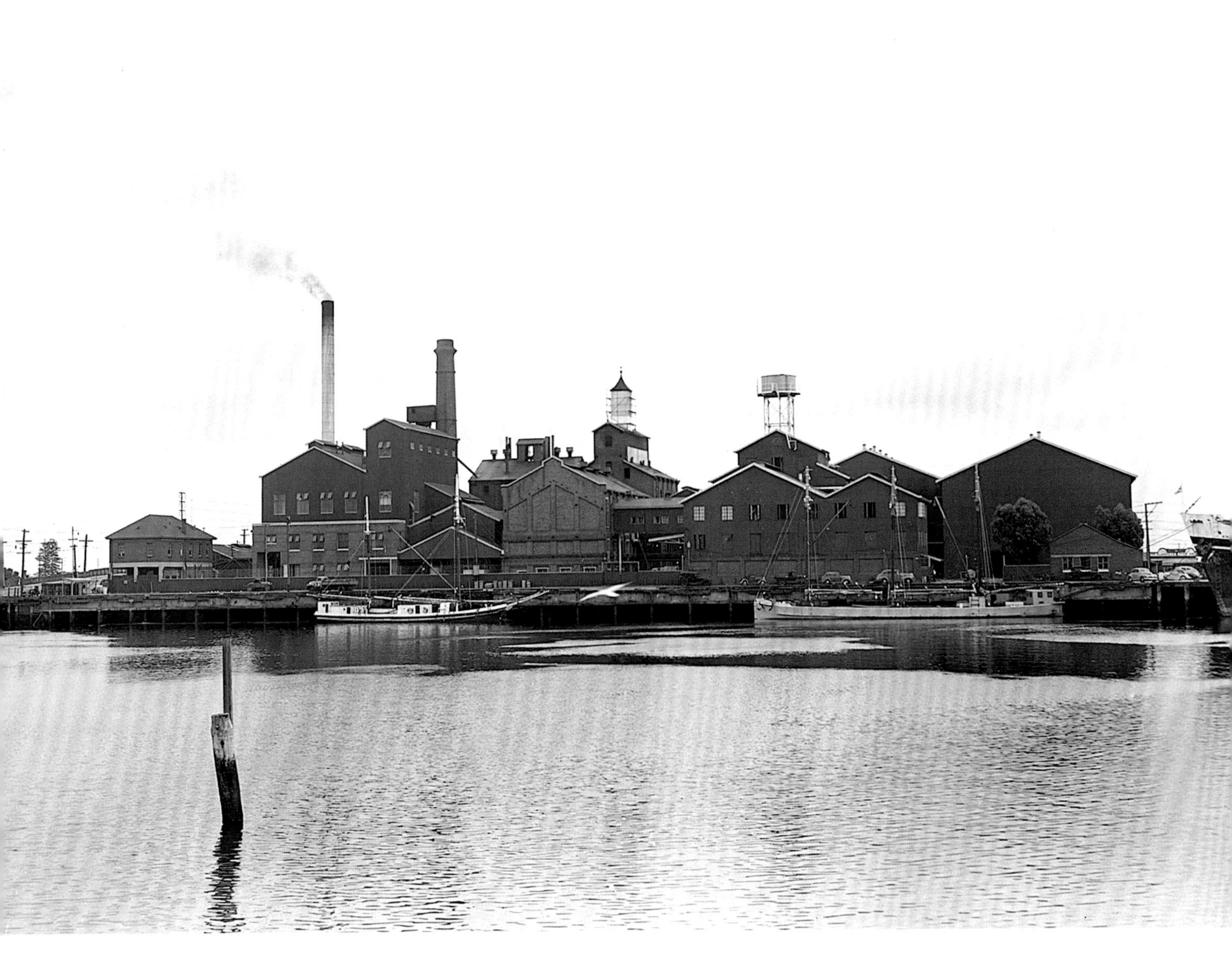

Above: Port Adelaide, Colonial Sugar Refinery. Demolished 1993, now Newport Quays.

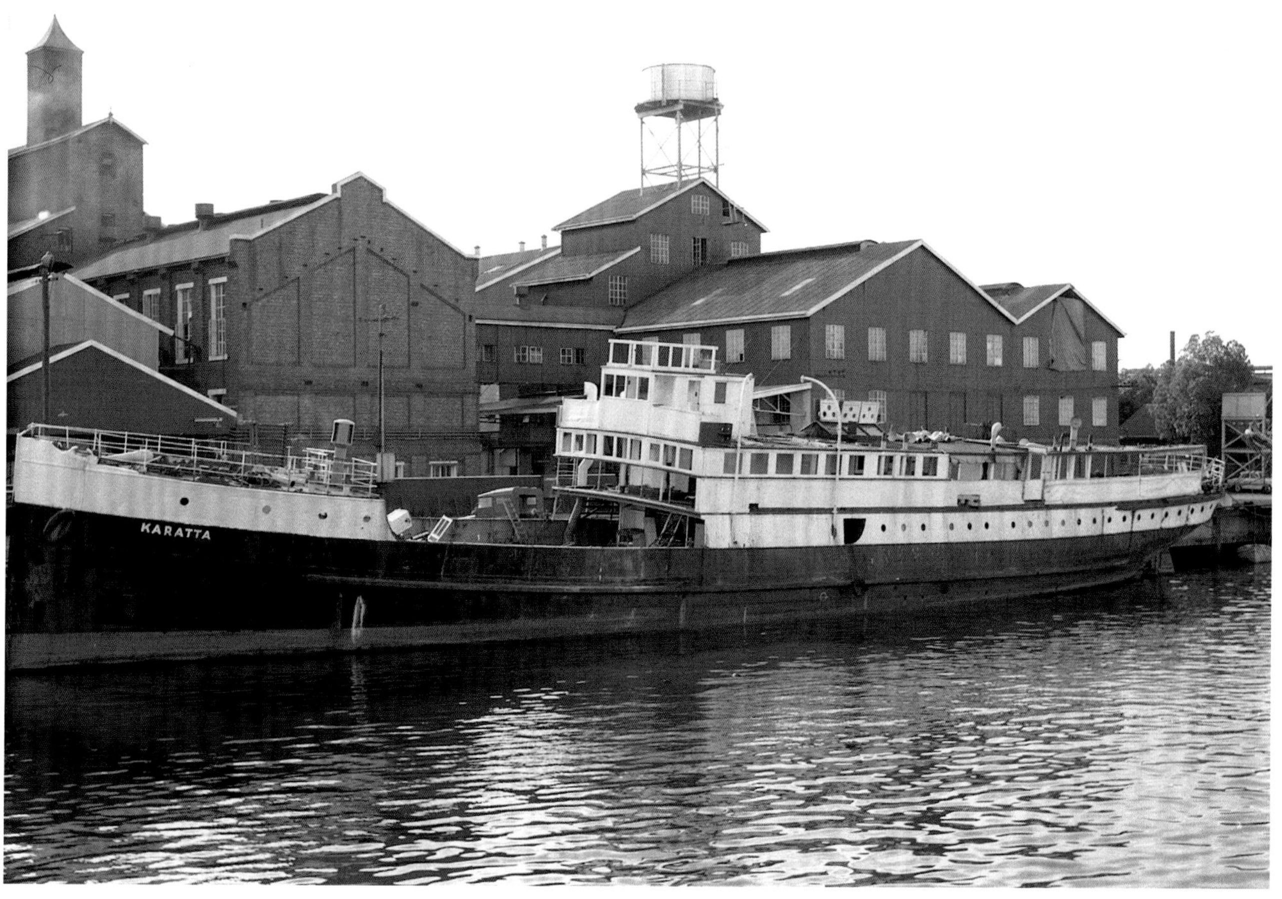

Above: *Karatta* going to scrap, Port Adelaide, 1961.

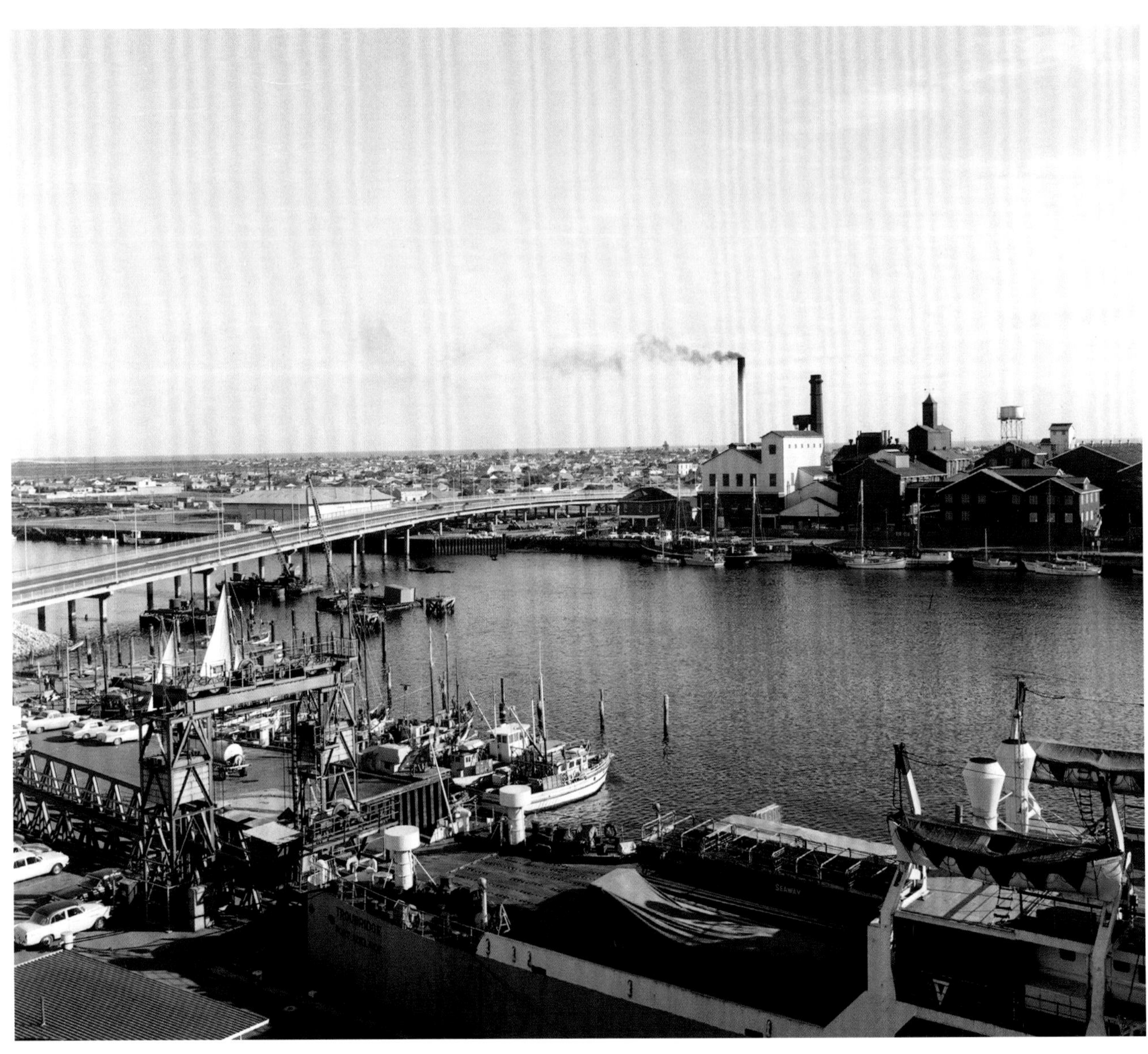

Above: Jervois Bridge and Colonial Sugar Refinery, *Troubridge* Kangaroo Island ship in the foreground, 1969.

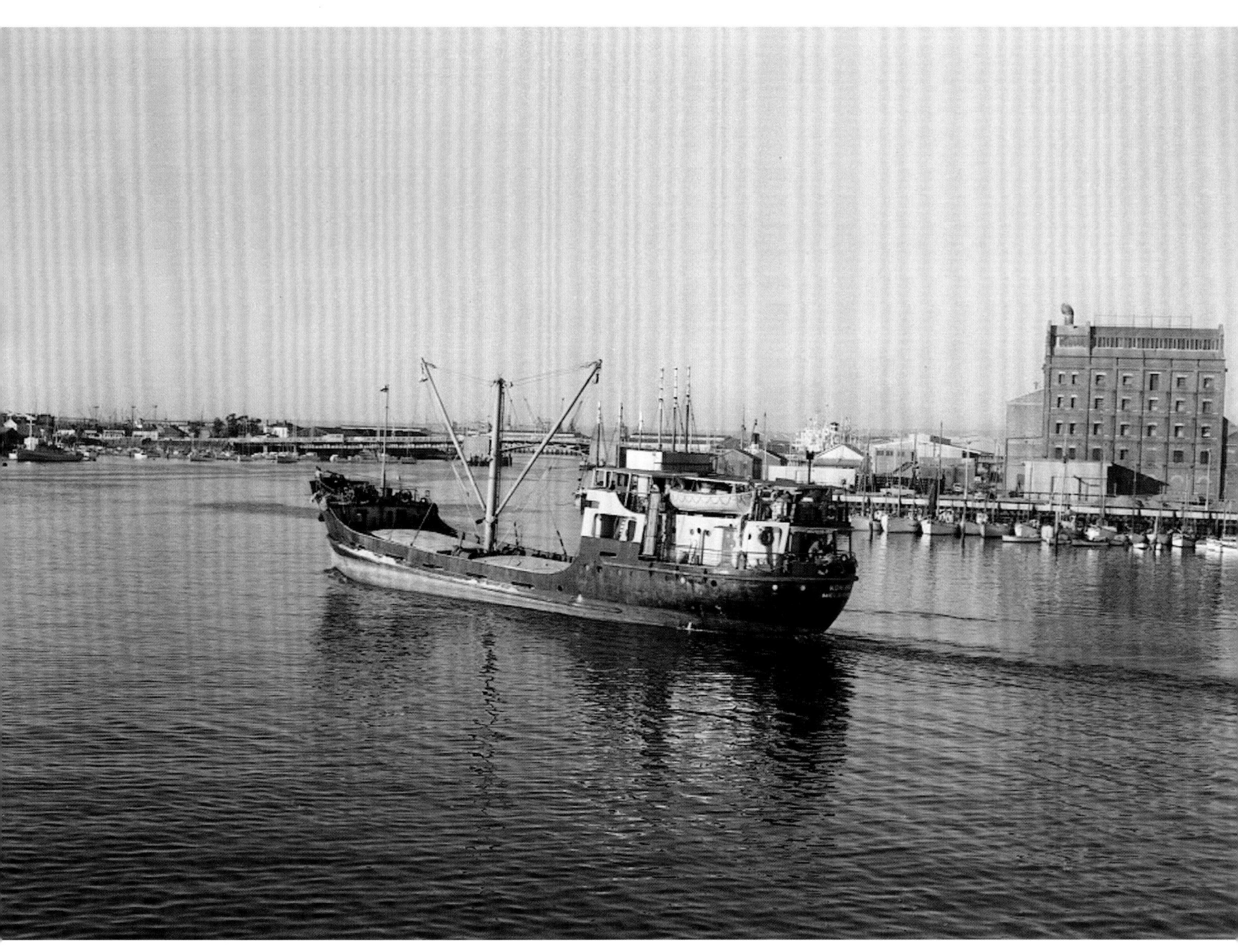

Above: Port River. The Adelaide Milling Company mill largely obscures the original Hart's Mill, 1960s.

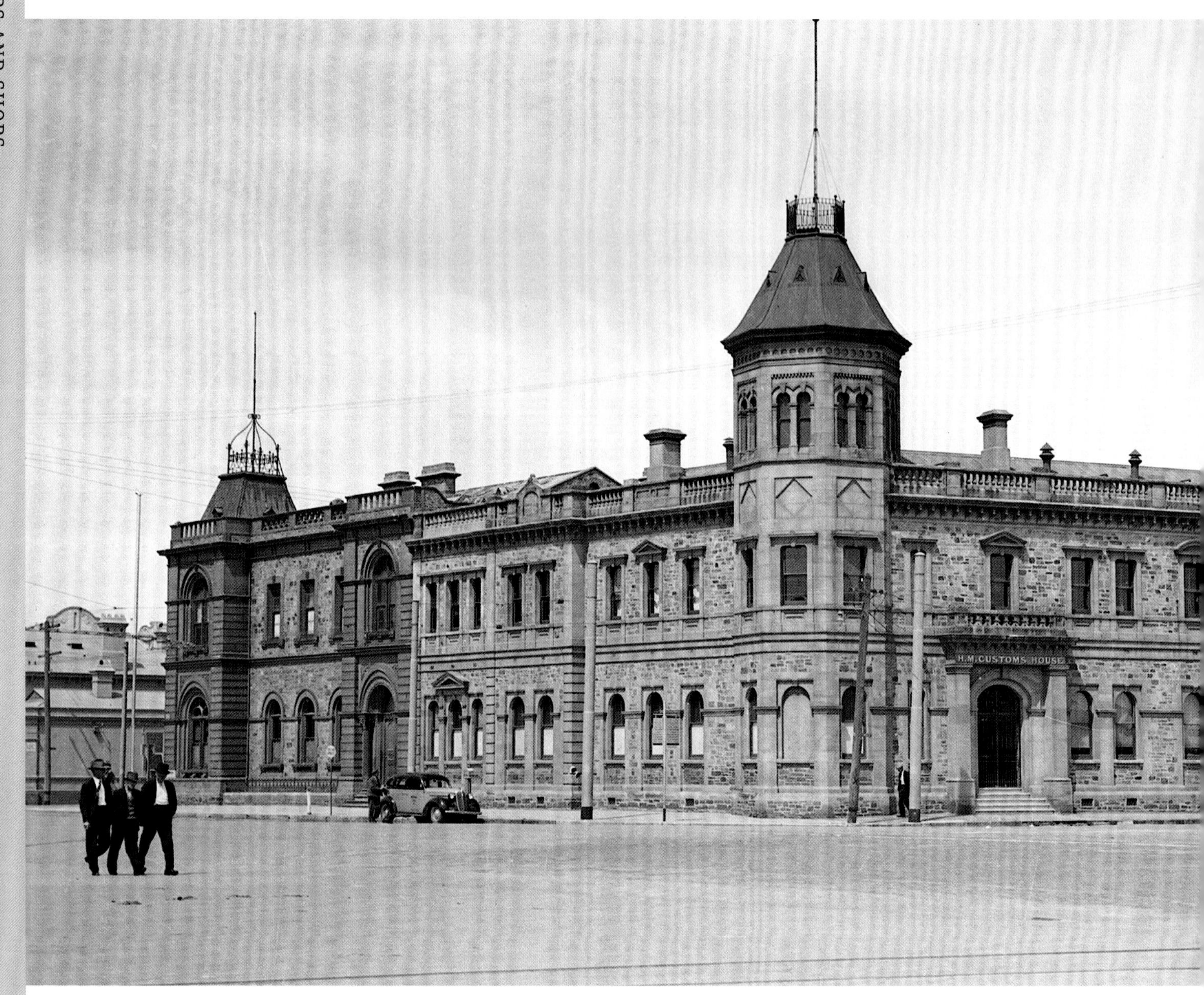

Above: Port Adelaide Institute and the Customs House, Port Adelaide, 1930s.

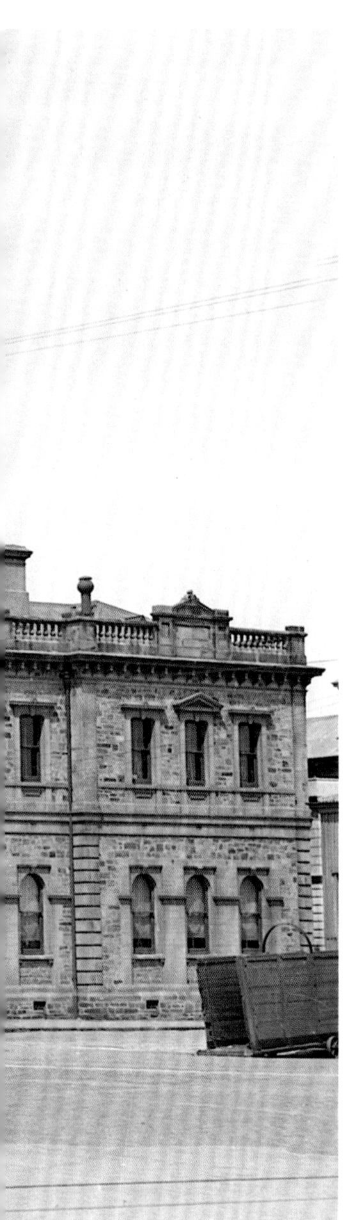

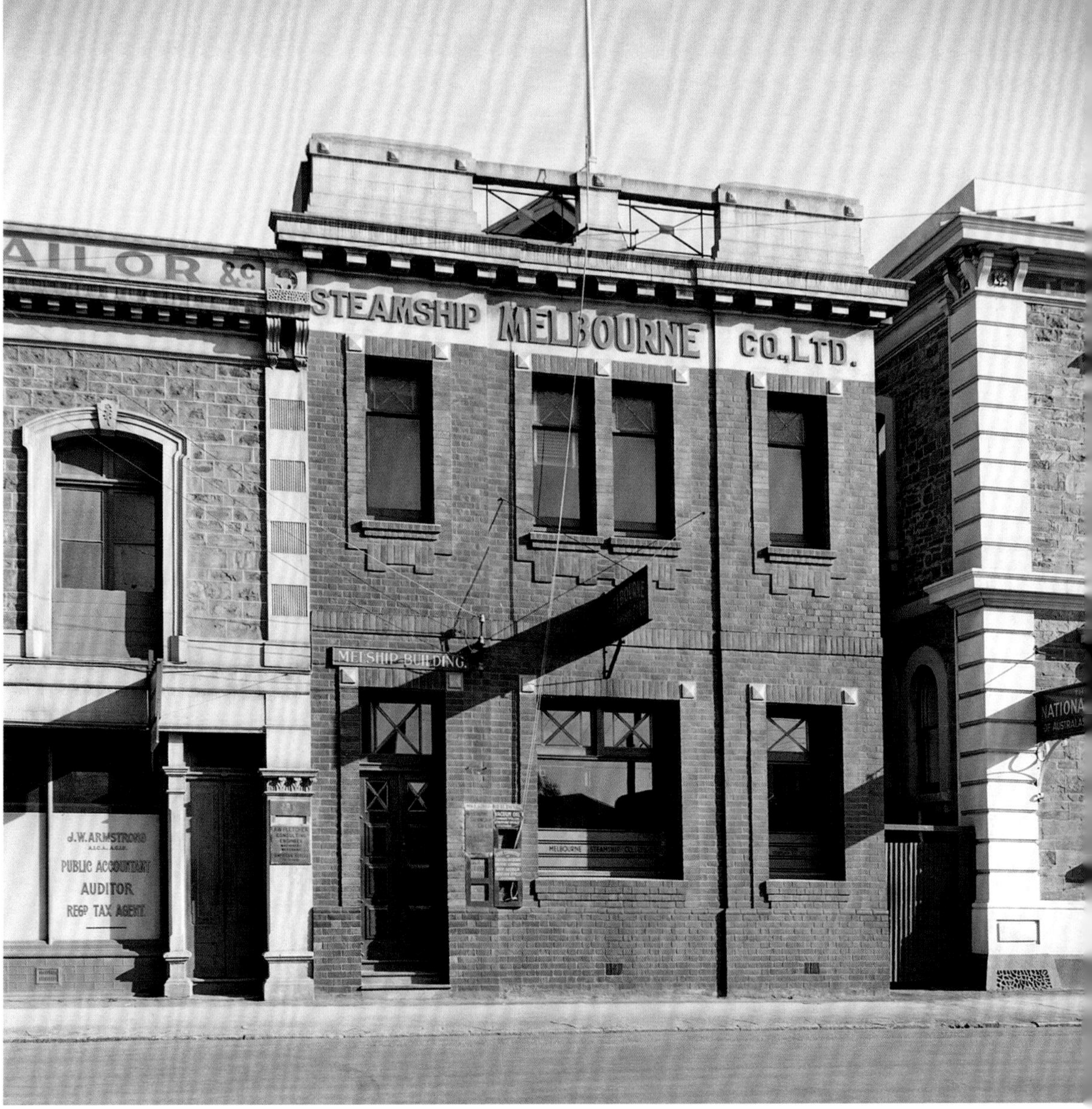

Above: Melbourne Steamship Company, Divett Street, Port Adelaide.

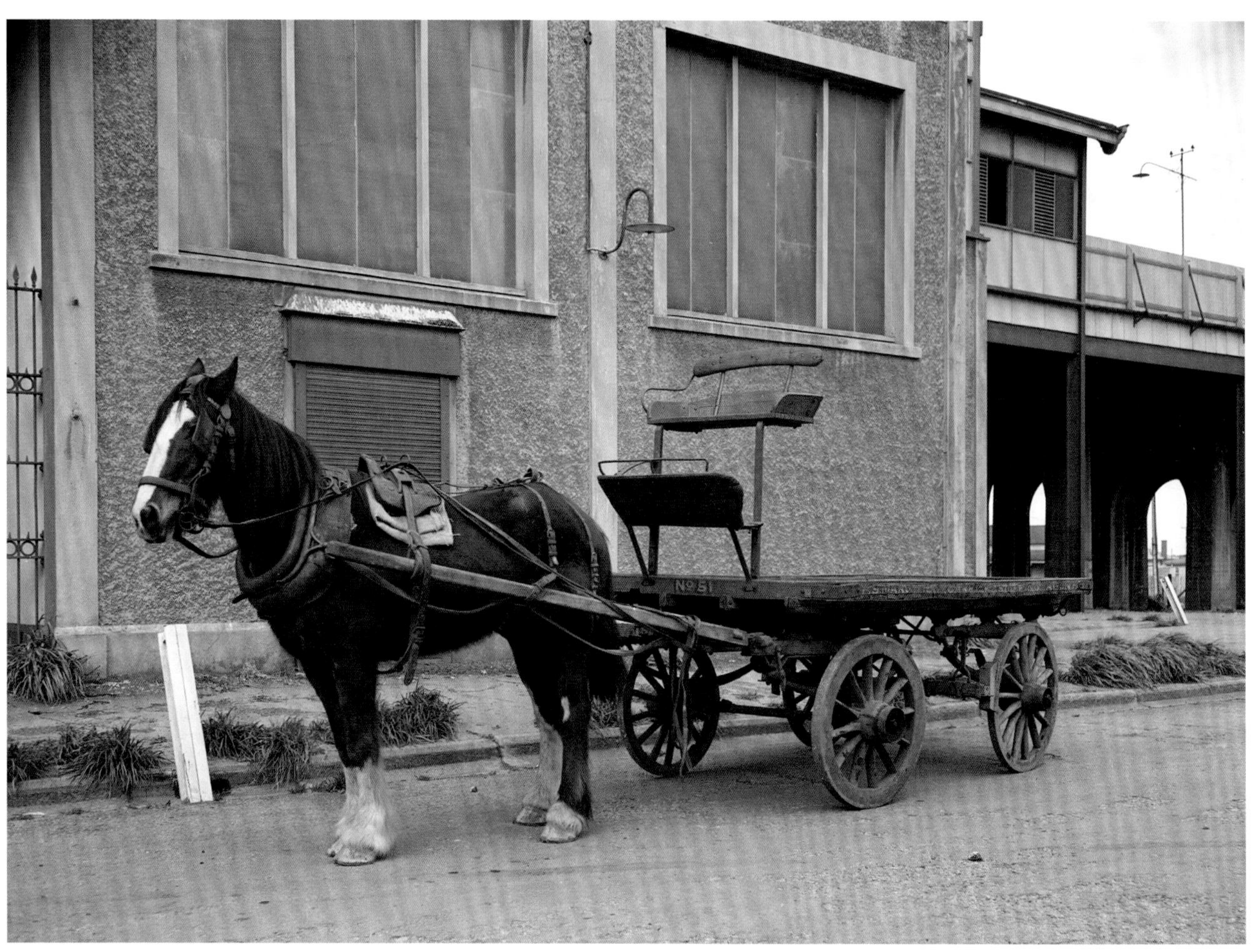

Above: Port Adelaide Margitich Carriers and Shipping Agents, early mode of transport.

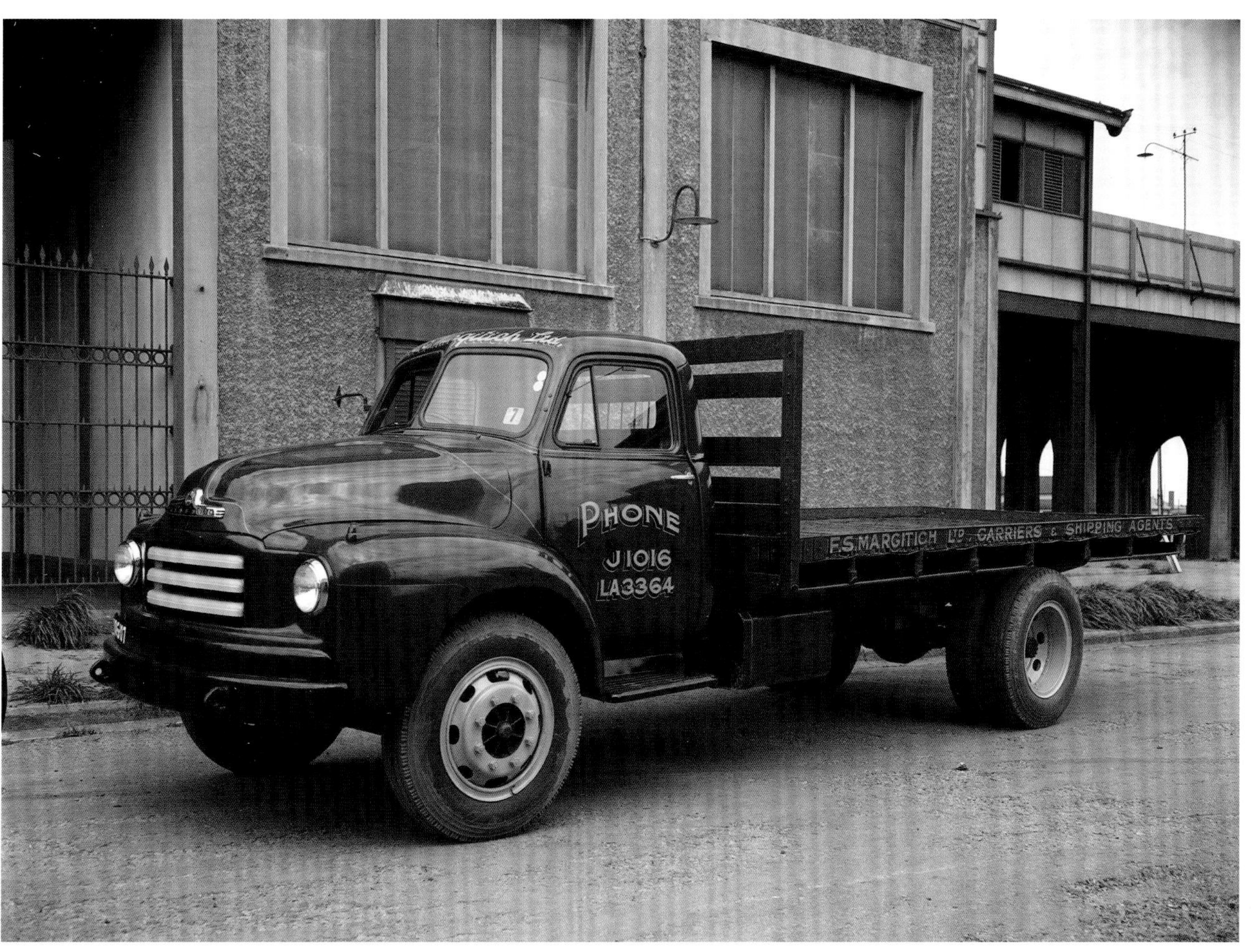

Above: The modern Margitich, form of transport, 1950s.

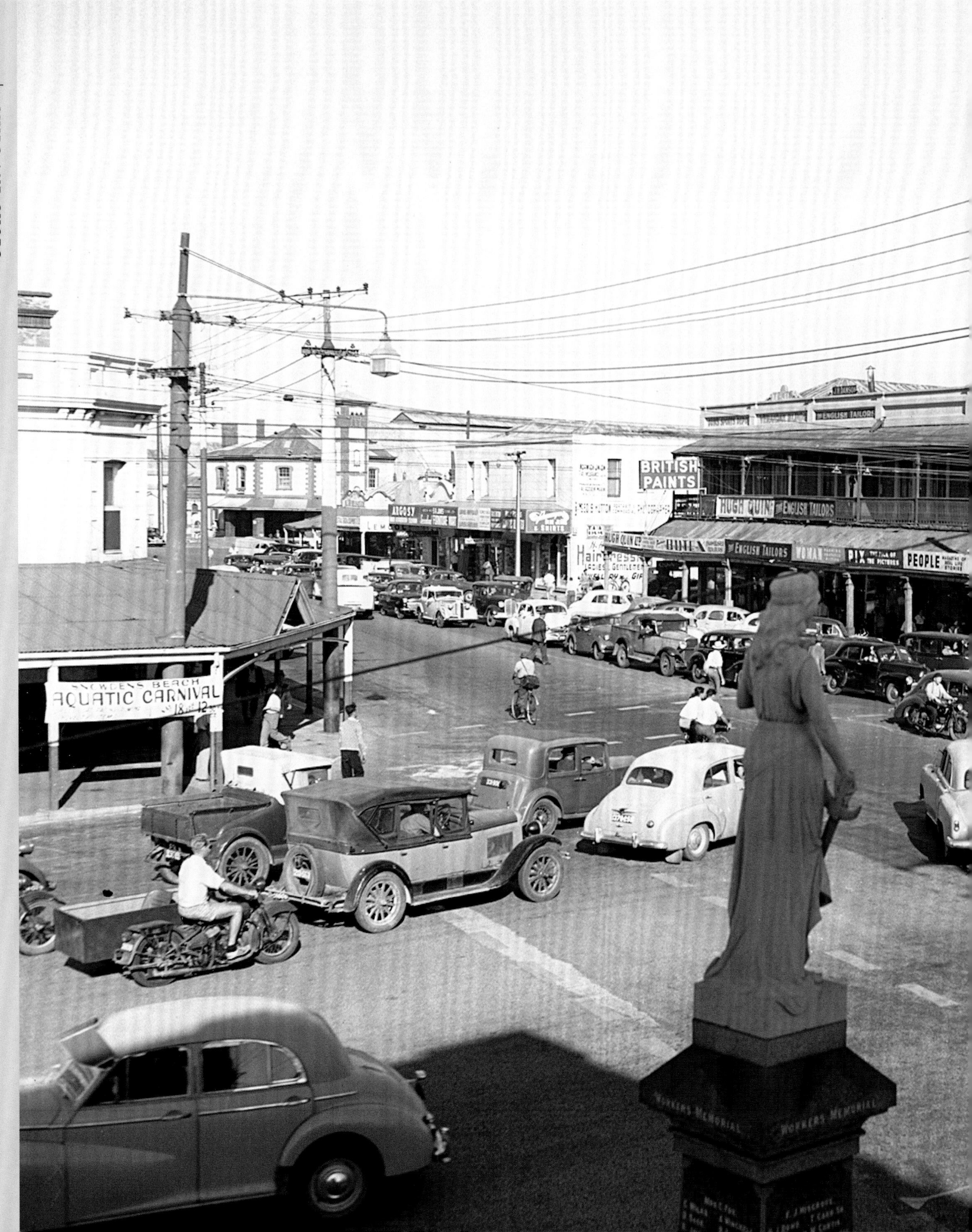
SNOWDENS BEACH
AQUATIC CARNIVAL
BRITISH PAINTS
HUGH QUIN
ENGLISH TAILORS
ARGOSY
PEOPLE
WORKERS MEMORIAL

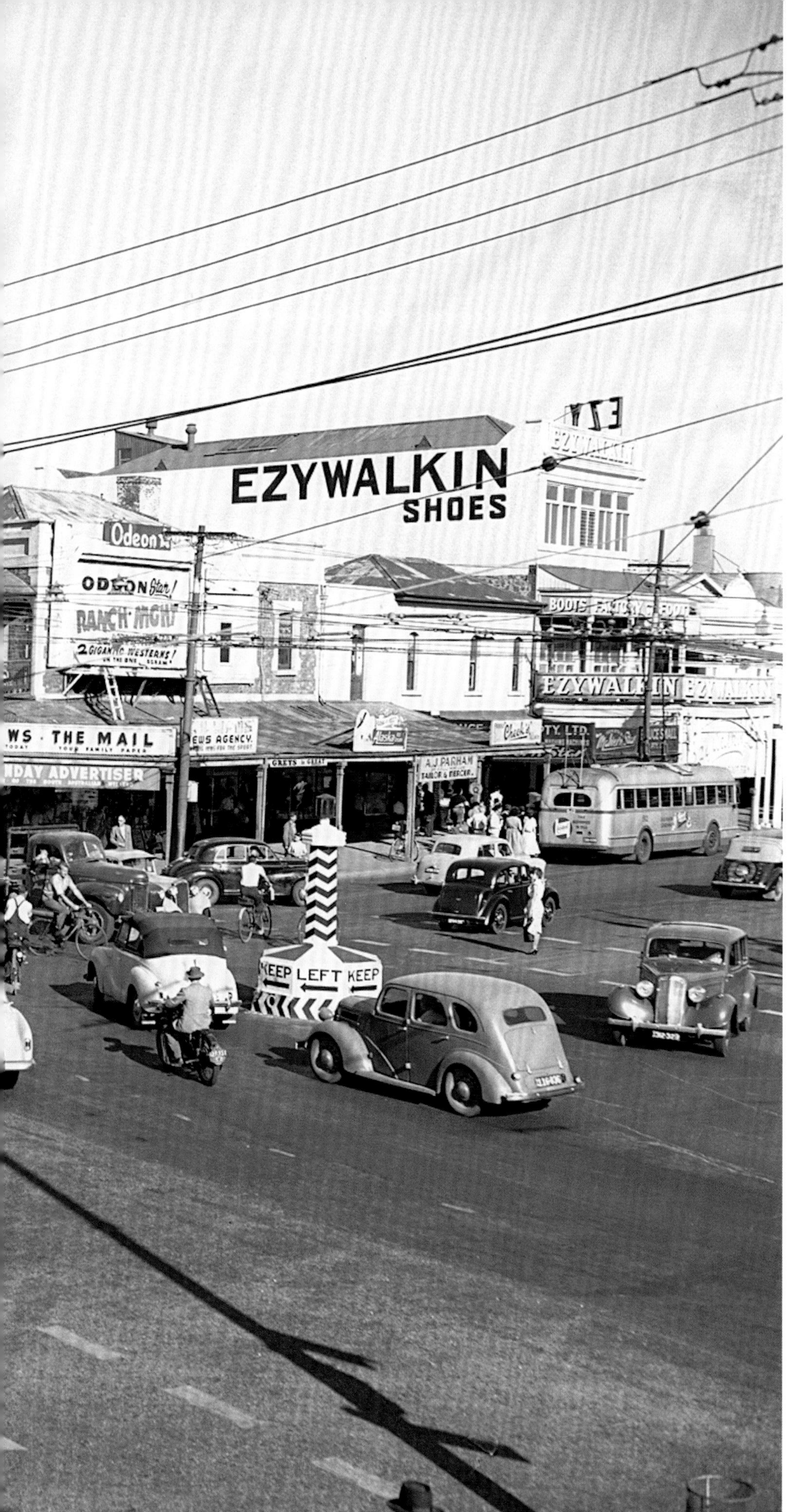

Left: Port Adelaide, Black Diamond, Corner Commercial Road and St Vincent Street, 1950s.

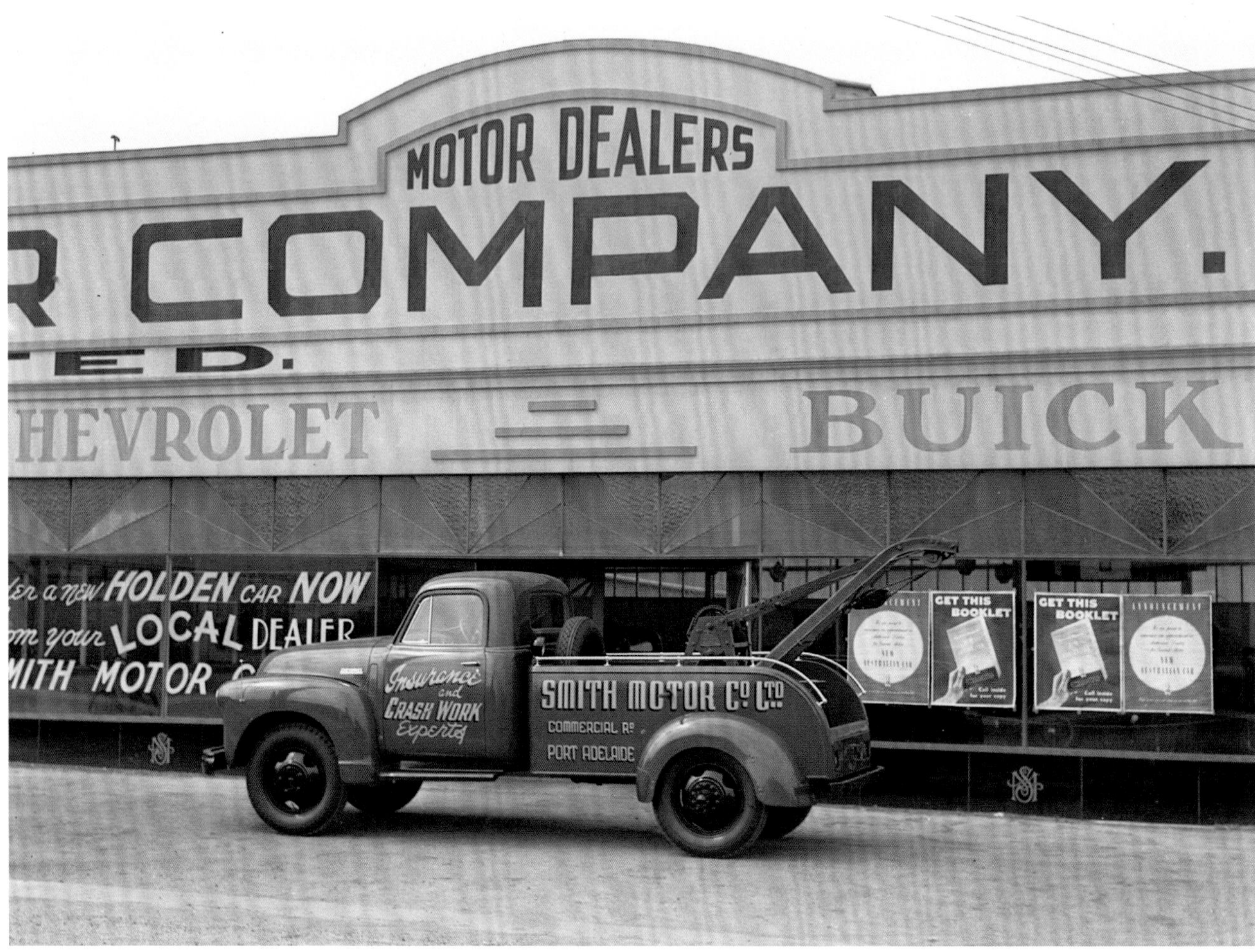

Above: Smith Motor Company, Commercial Road, Port Adelaide, 1950s.

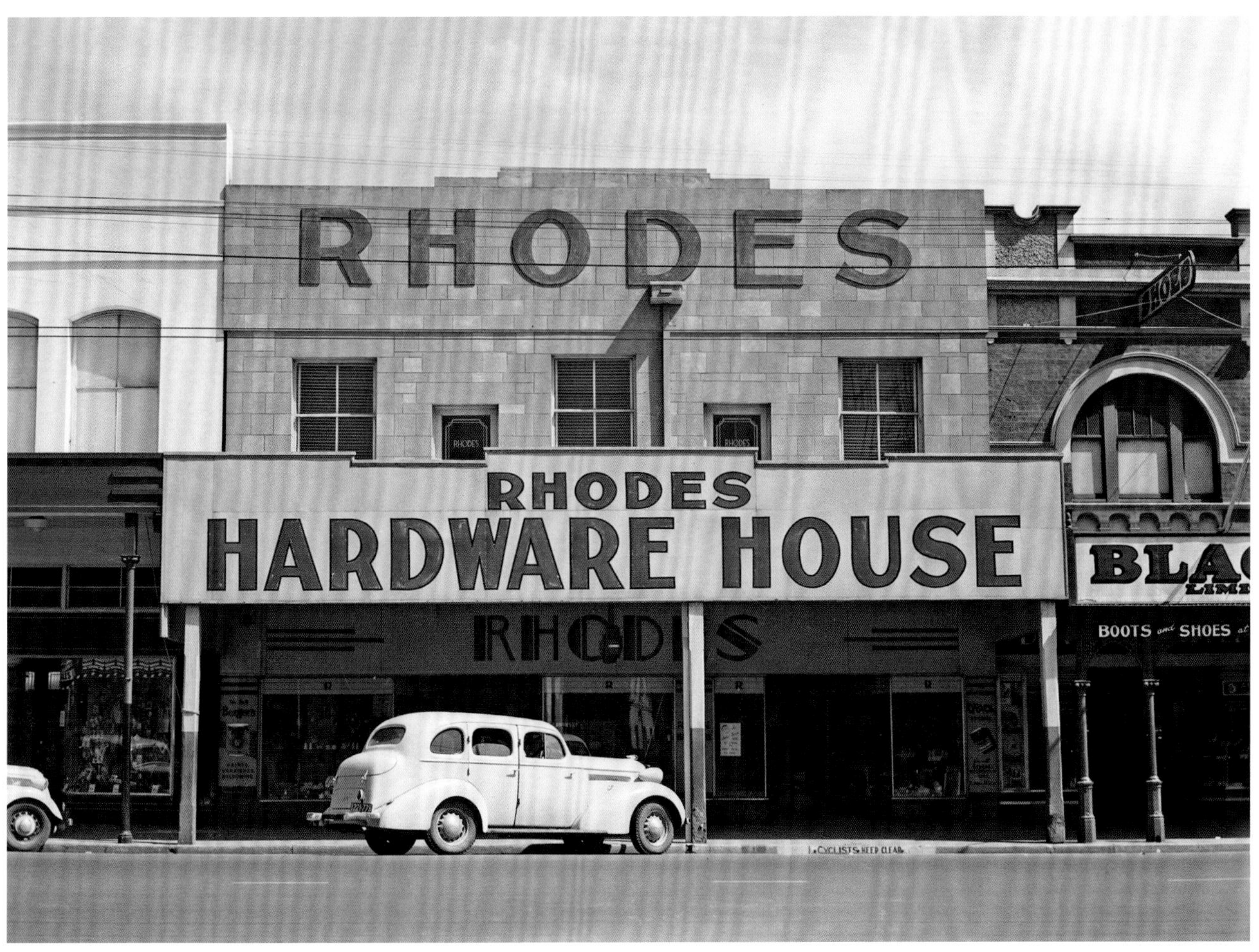

Above: Rhodes, a landmark hardware shop in St Vincent Street, Port Adelaide, 1950s.

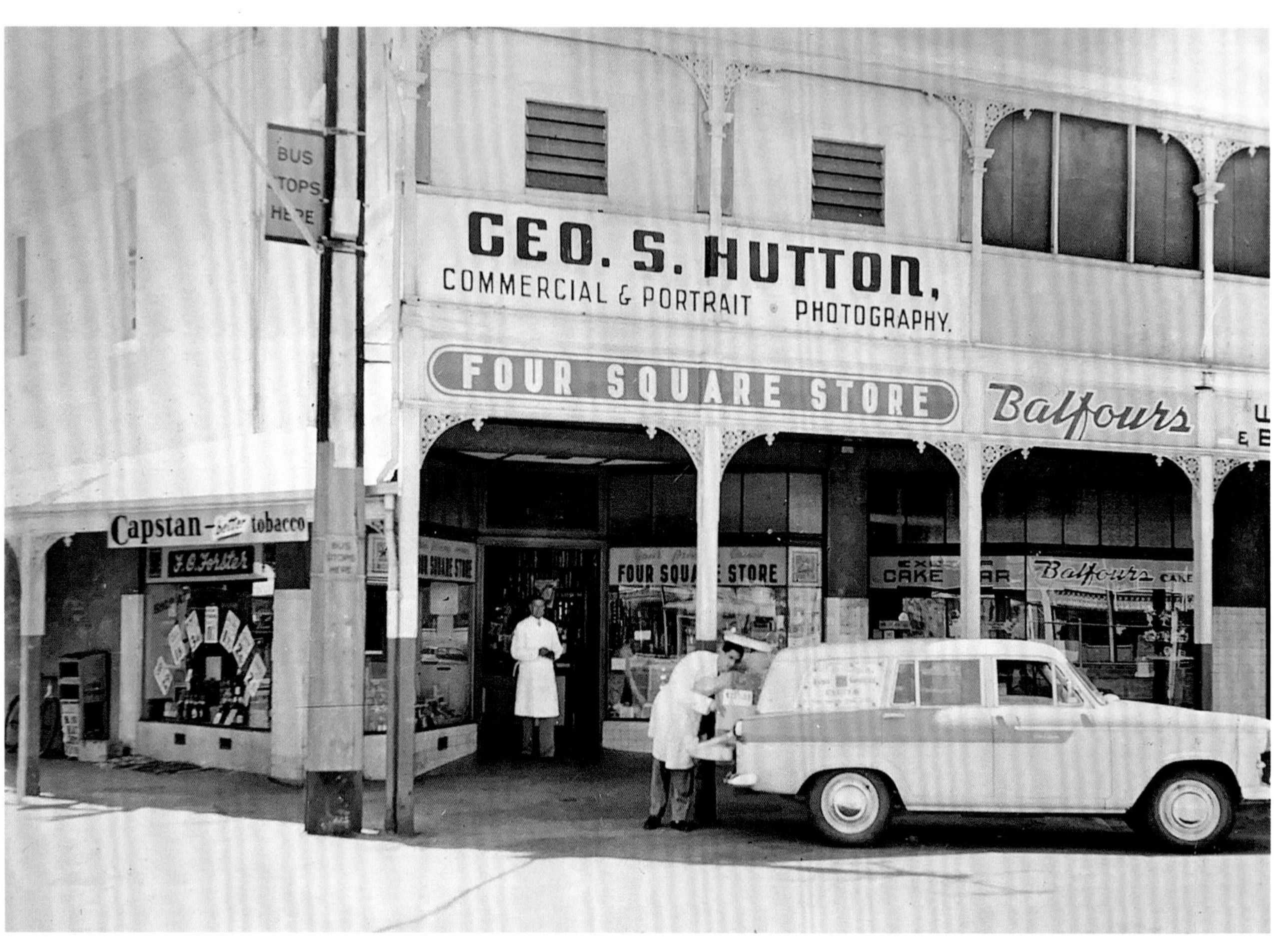

Above: Studio, Semaphore Road, Exeter, 1955.

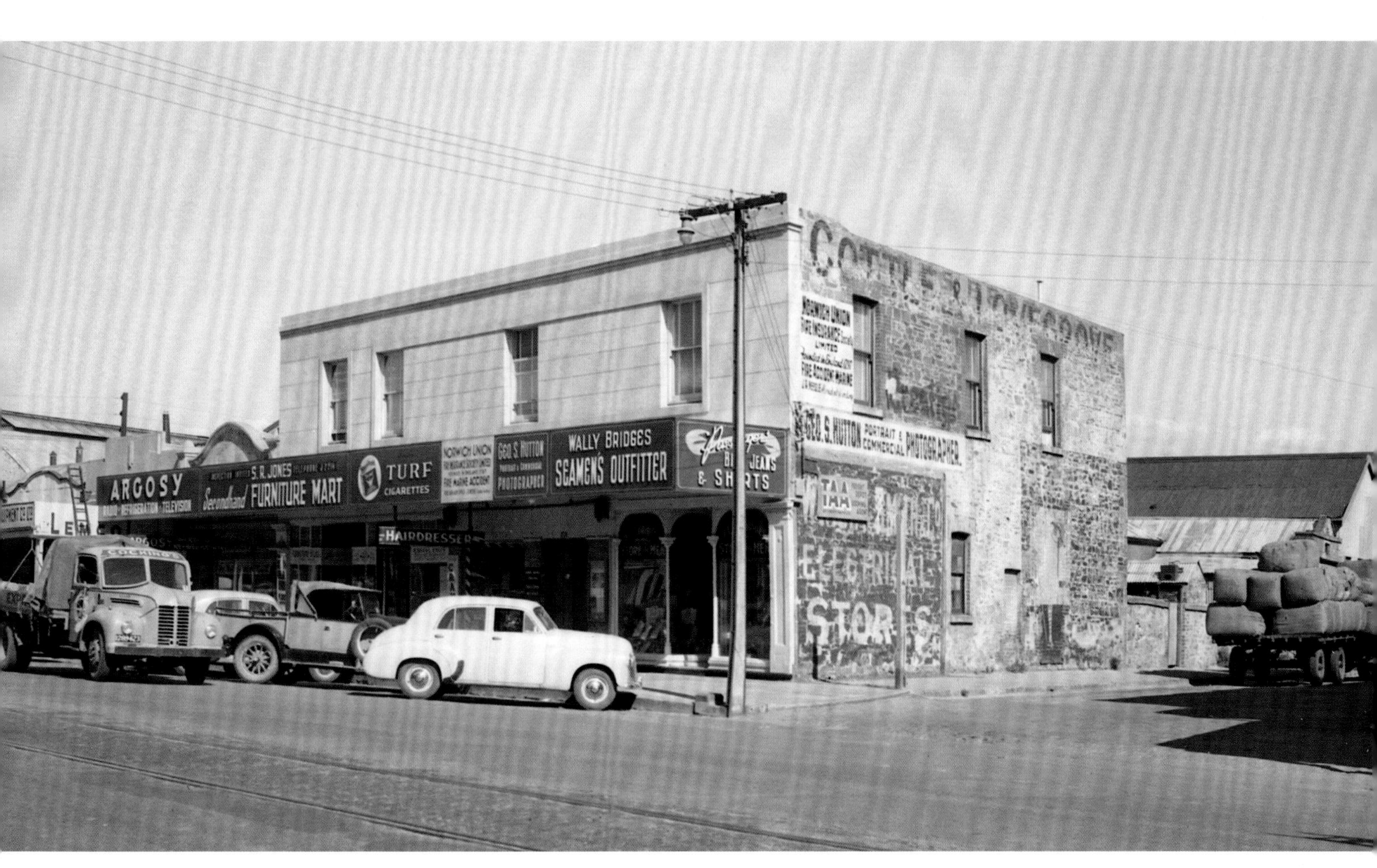

Above: Port Adelaide studio,
St Vincent Street, 1954.

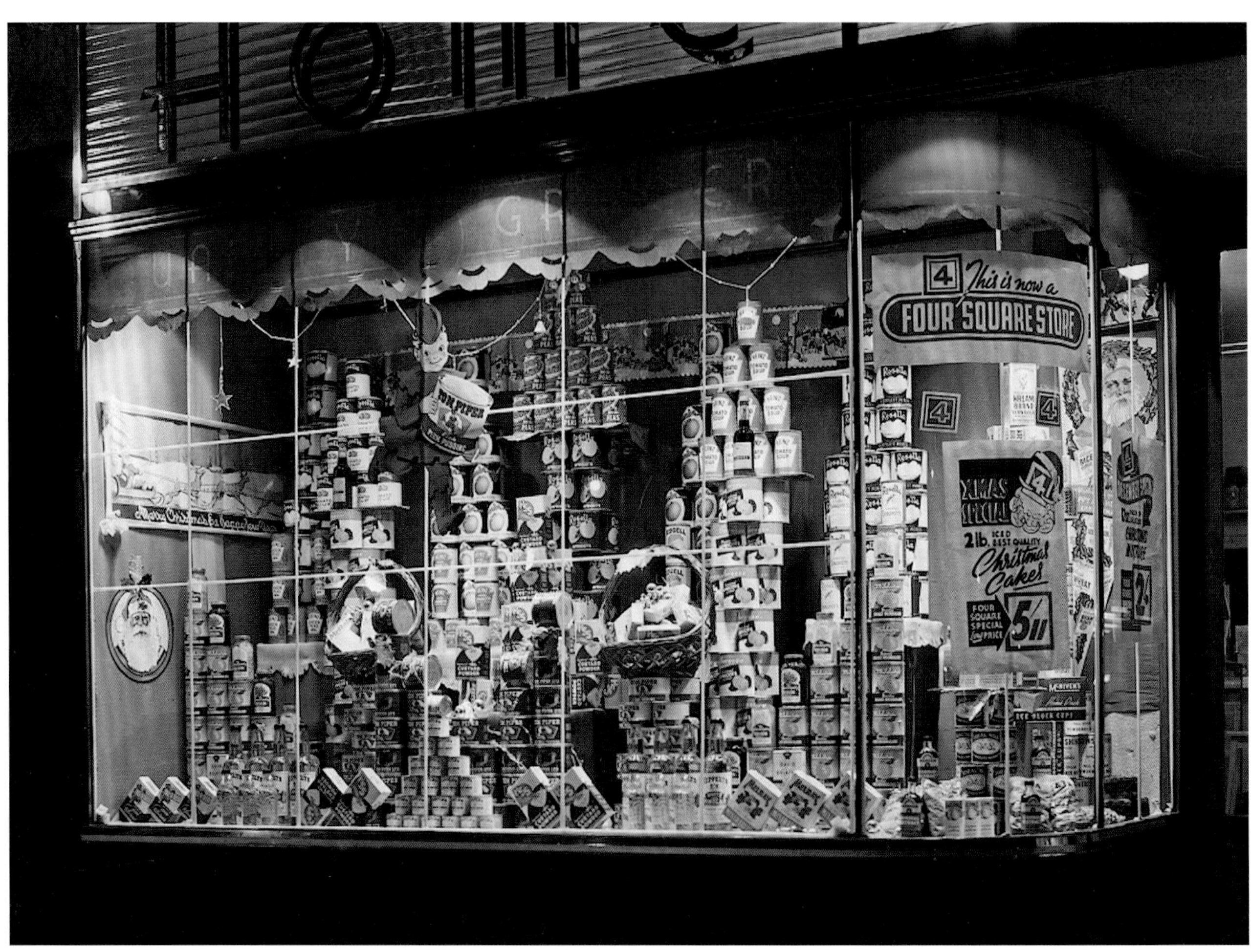

Above: Four Square Store, window display, Semaphore Road, 1959.

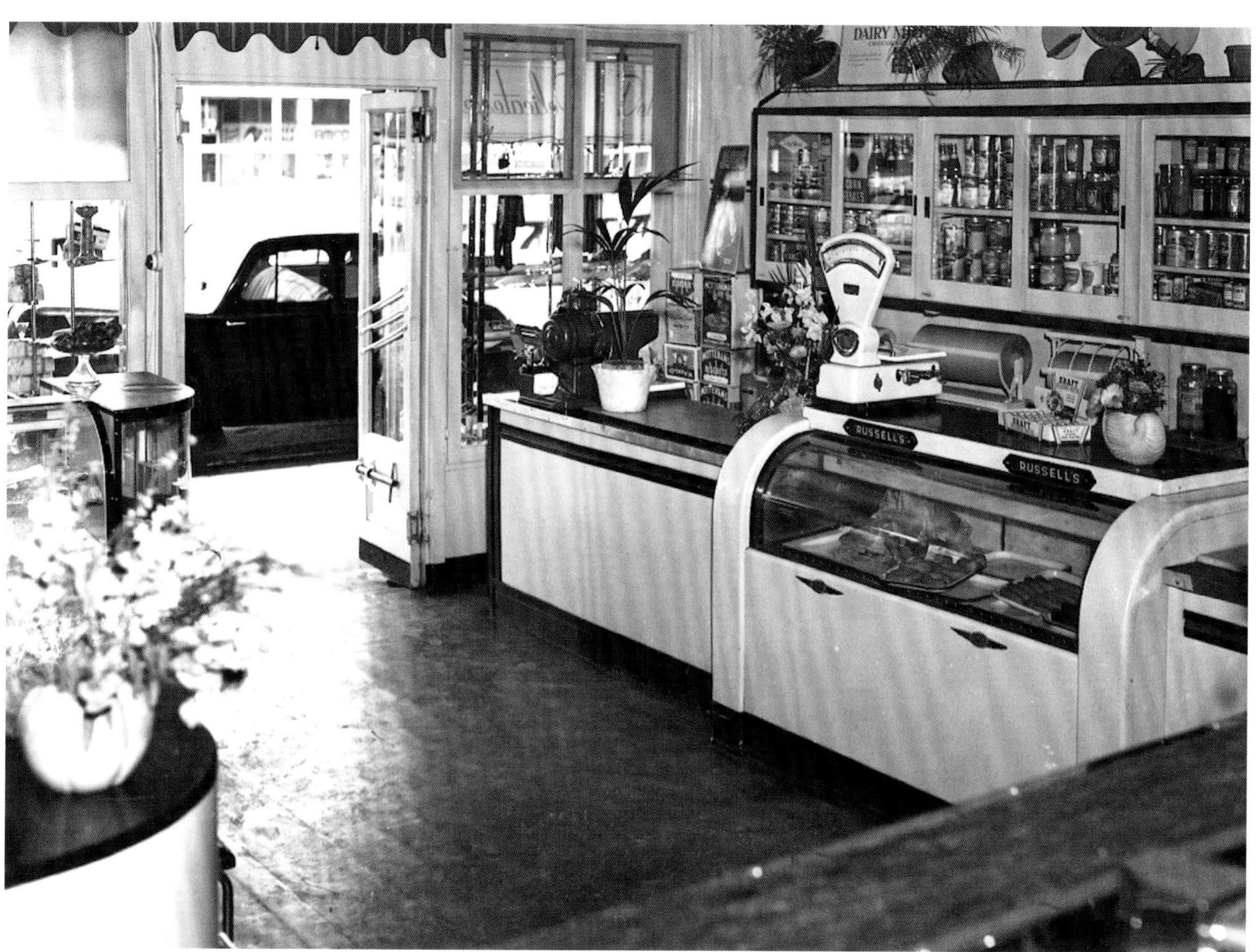

Above: J. Russell's shop, interior, Semaphore Road, 1950s.

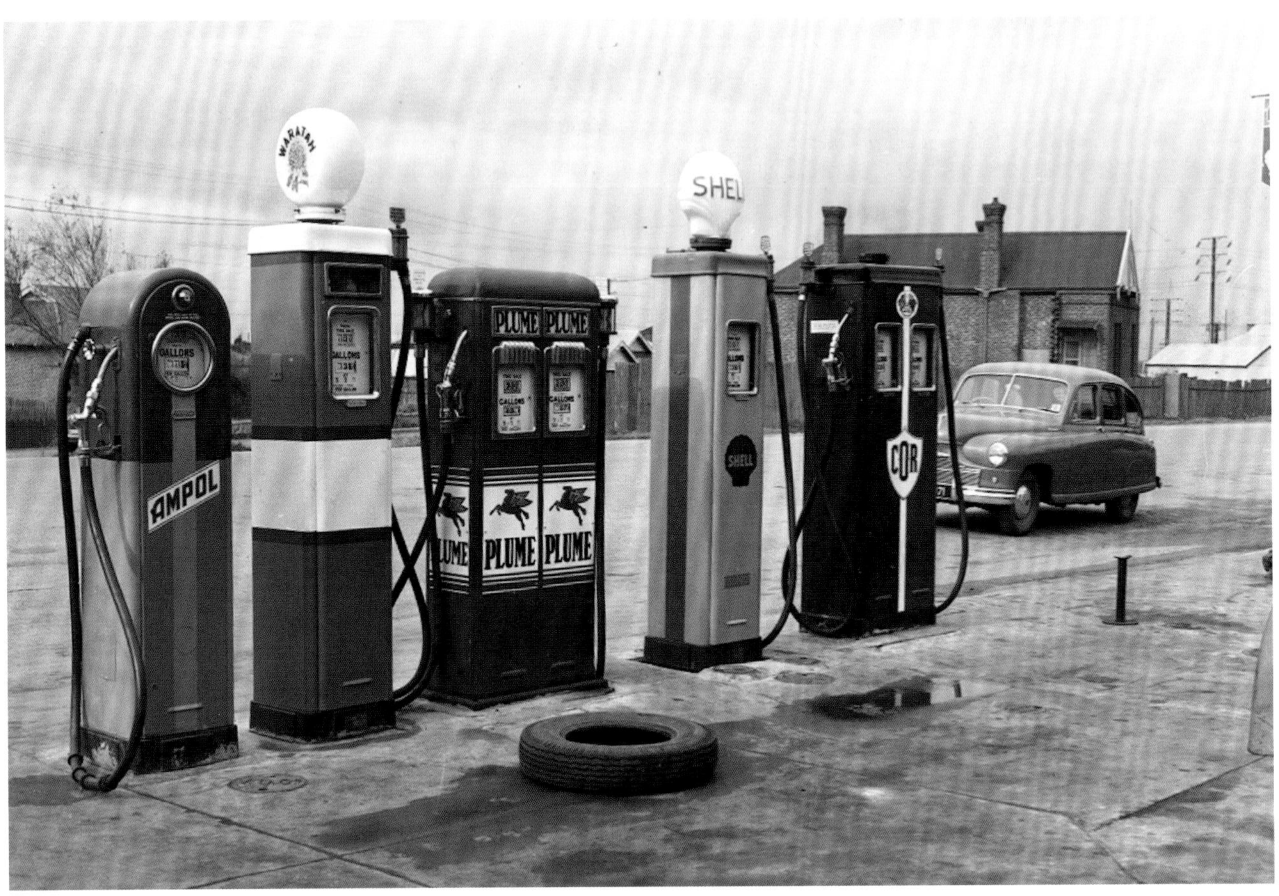

Above: Foster's Garage and George's Vanguard, 1959.

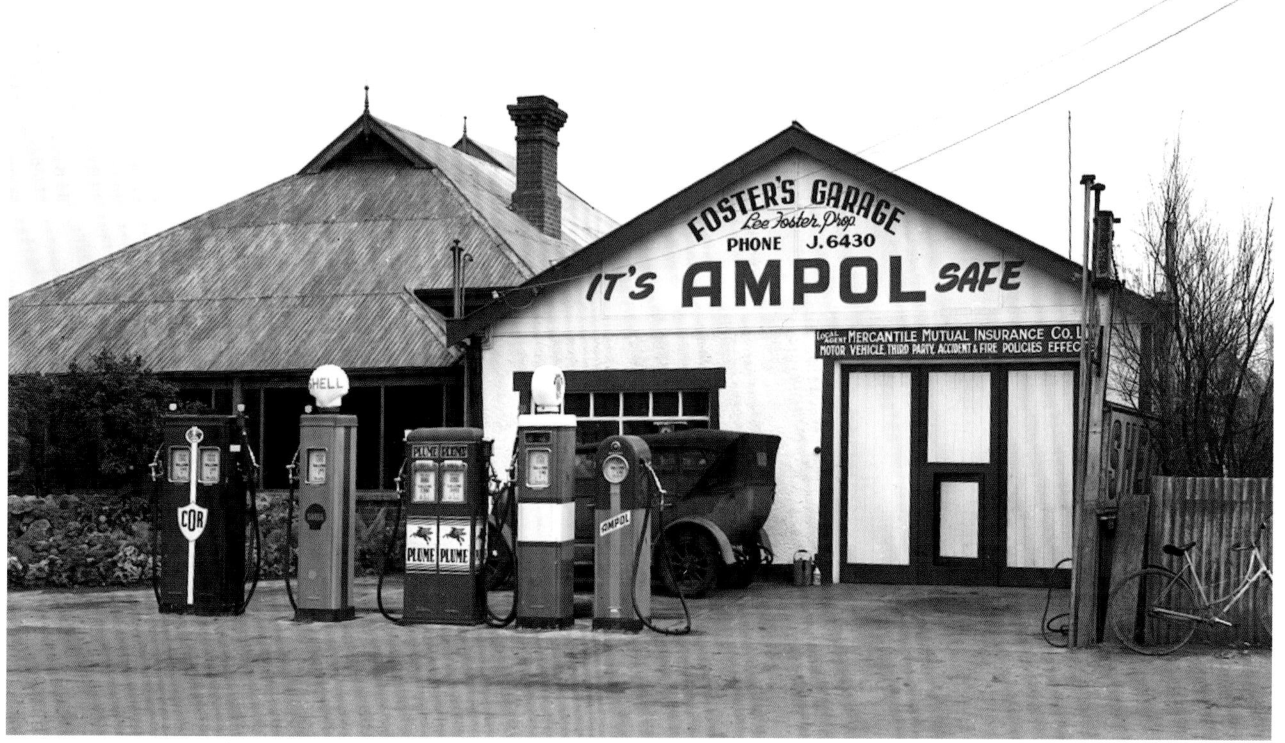

Above: Foster's Garage, Military Road, Largs North, 1959.

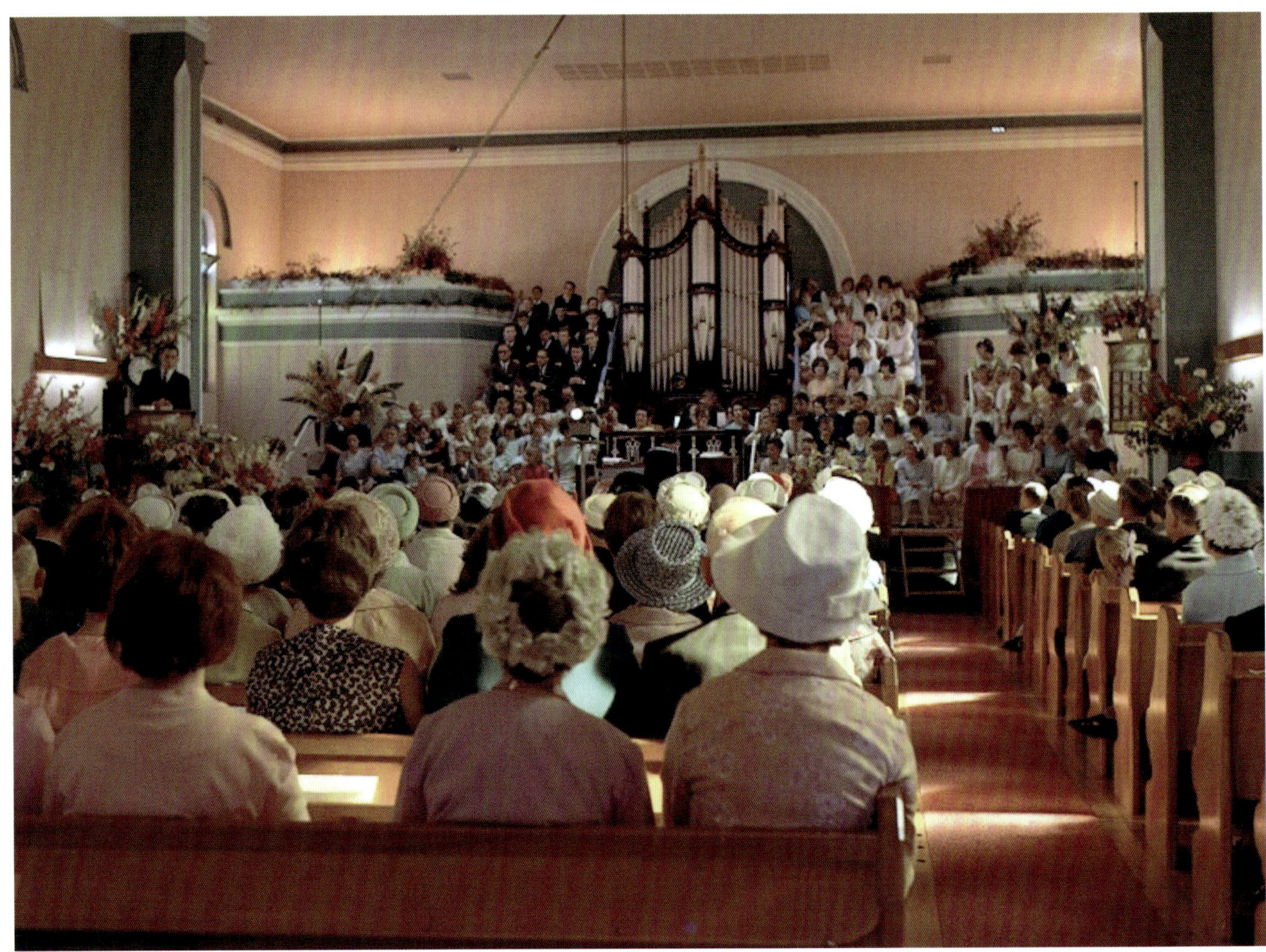

Above: Semaphore Baptist Church Anniversary 1967, son Deane Hutton is lay preaching.

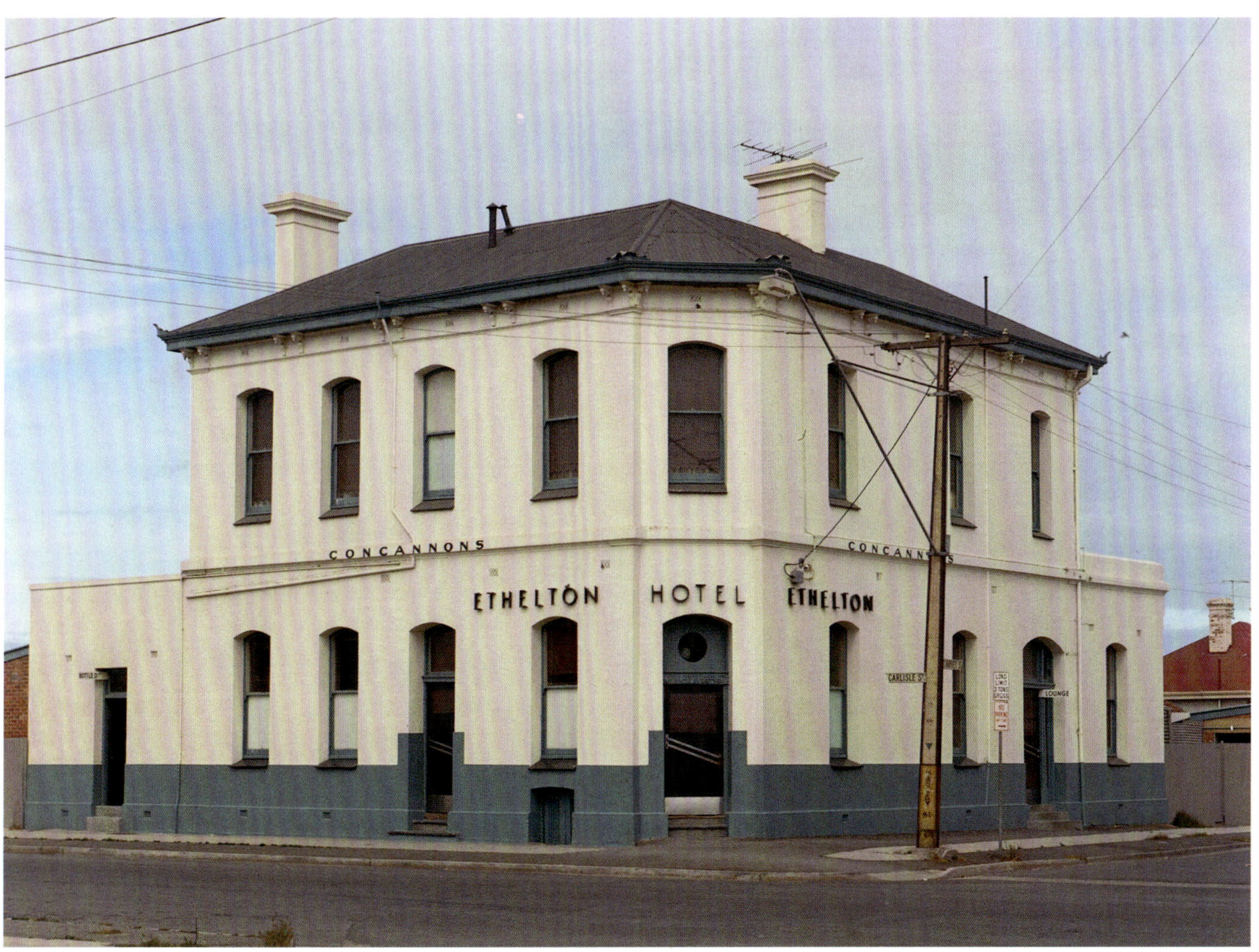

Above: Ethelton Hotel, 1960s. Since demolished. As a lifelong teetotaller, George did not approve of 'hard liquor', as he called it and only frequented public houses when he attended meetings of his Rotary Club.

BEACHES AND BEAUTIES

George often photographed seaside scenes in the beach suburbs of Semaphore and Largs Bay, where he lived and worked – from a tent-covered Semaphore seashore on a hot summer's day, to sandcastle competitions and bathing beauties.

George lived at Semaphore, Ethelton and Largs Bay. He often enjoyed swimming in the warmer months, carefully placing his spectacles in the Velcro pocket of his grey towel.

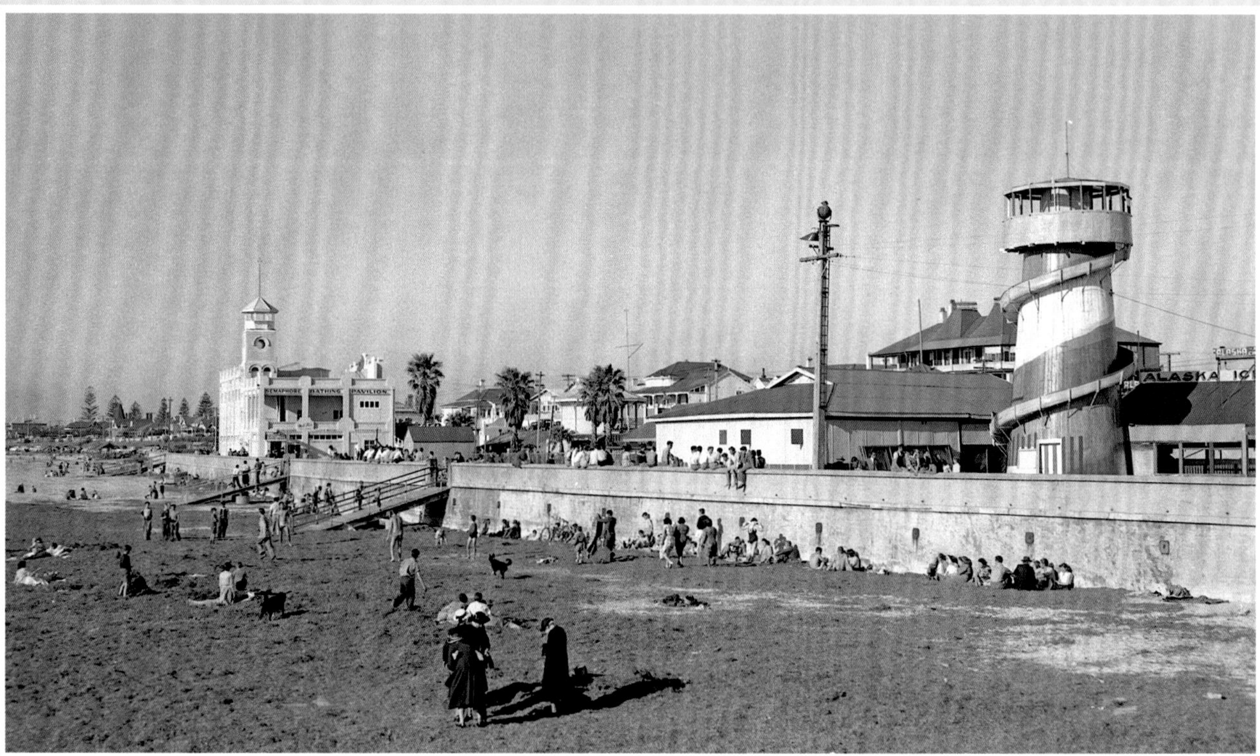

Above: Seagrass-covered Semaphore beach, showing the Palais and seawall, 1950s.
Opposite: Miss Semaphore, 1932
Following spread: Crowded beach, taken from the Semaphore jetty. The only remaining buildings are the Palais (extreme left), Wondergraph Café (to the left of the Wondergraph Pictures and later known as Evancourt Private Hotel), the house behind it, Evancourt (behind the refreshment shed) and the Customs House and Semaphore Hotel (behind the carousel), 1924.

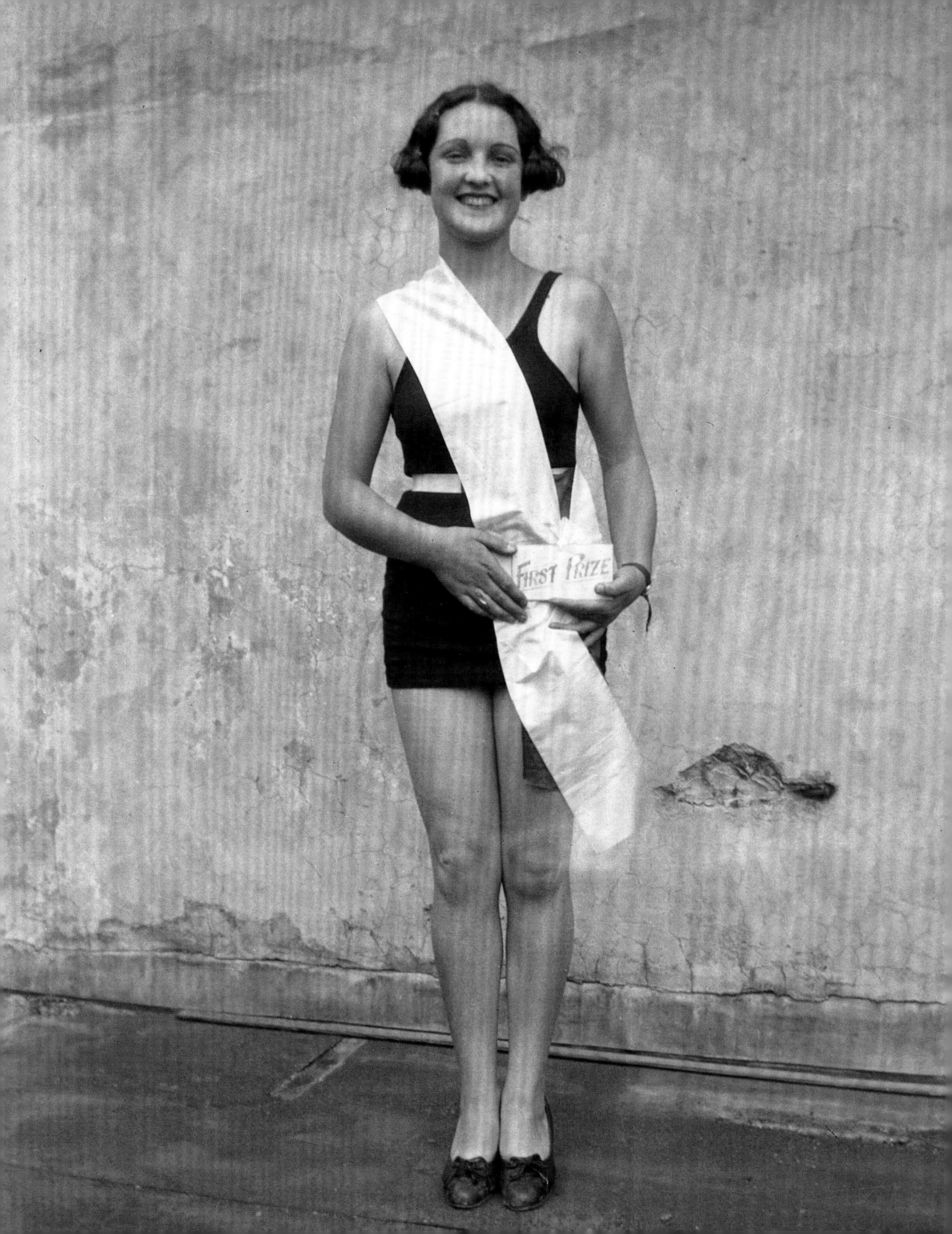
FIRST PRIZE

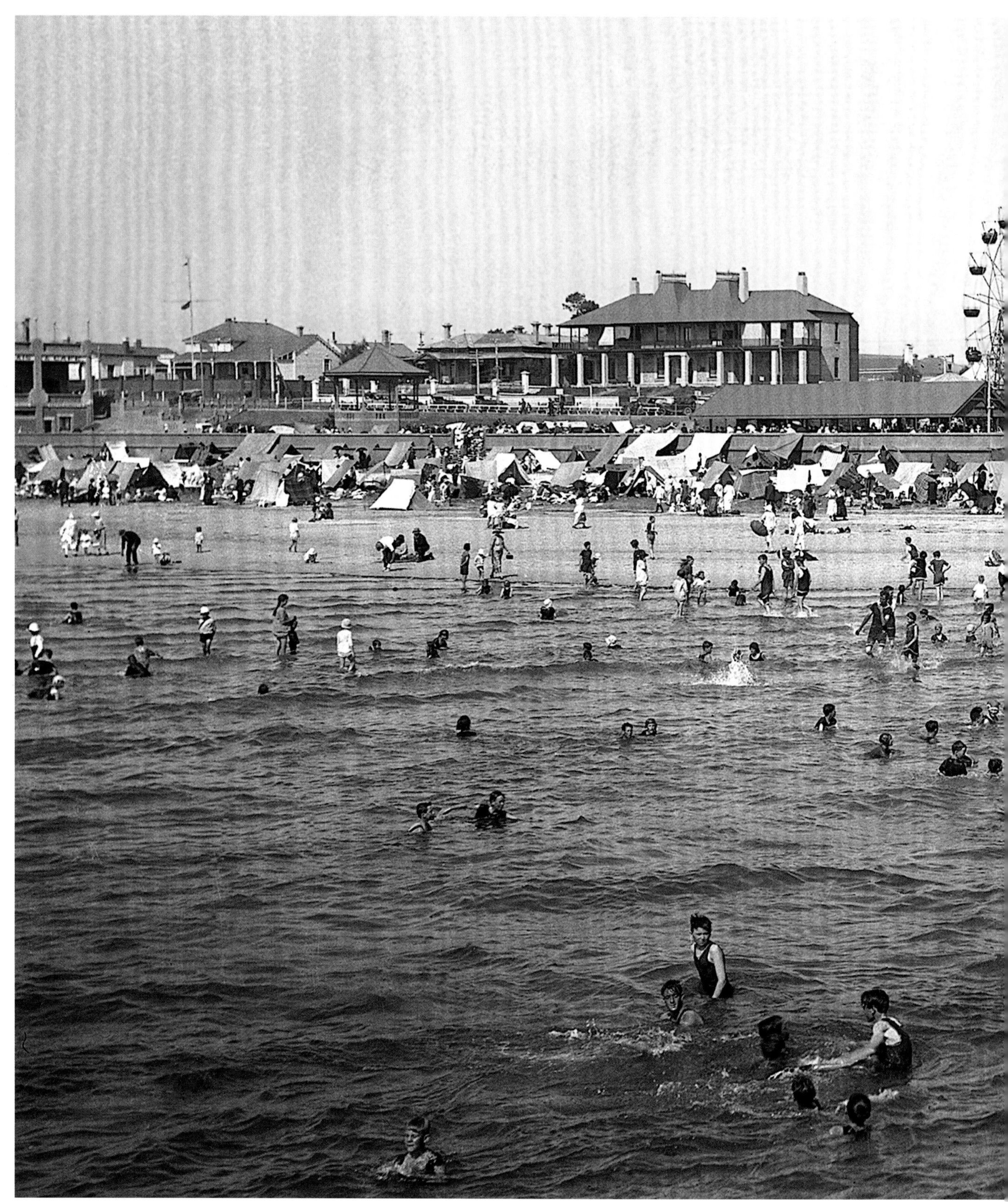

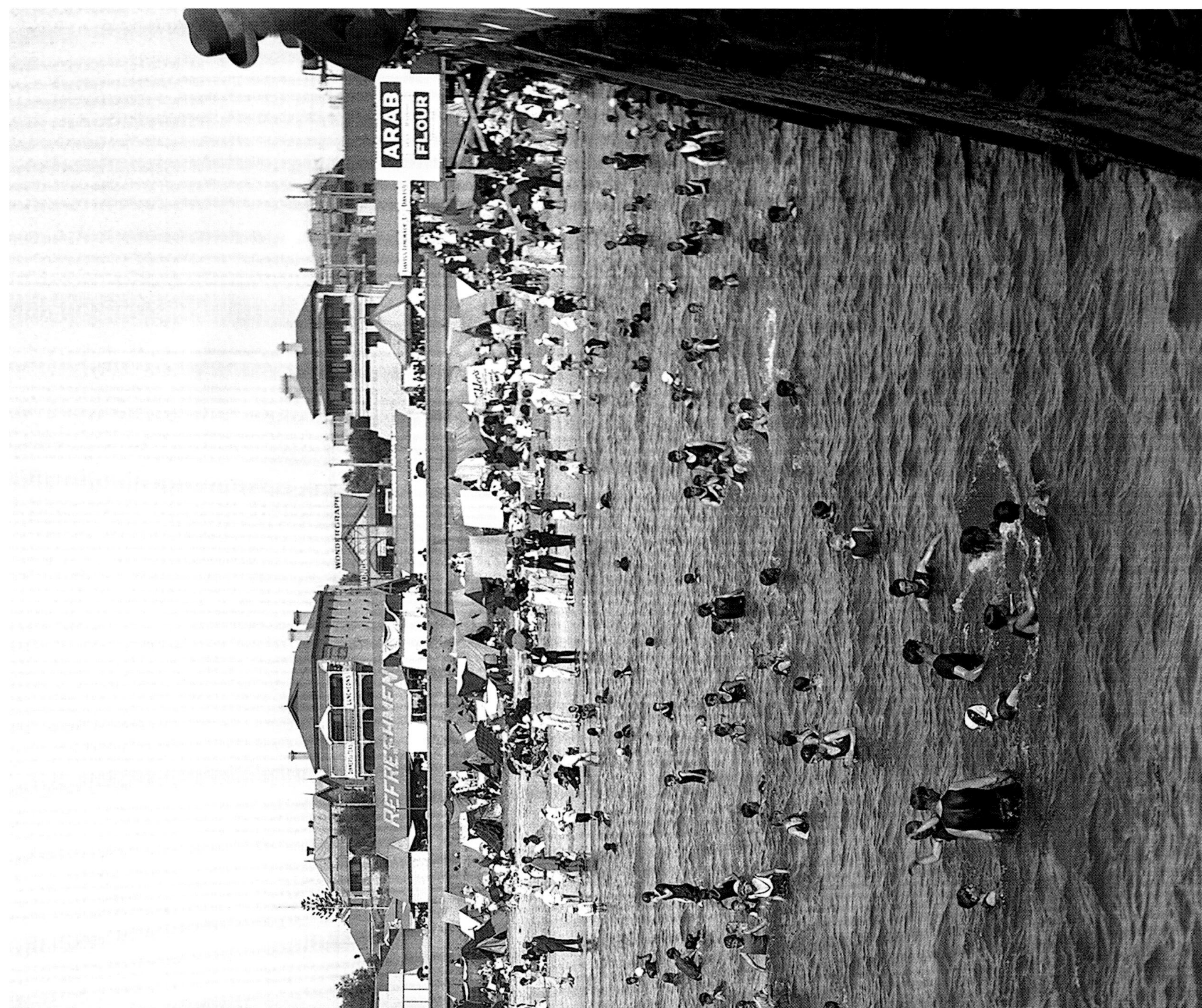
ARAB
FLOUR
WONDERGRAPH
LUNCHEONS
REFRESHMEN

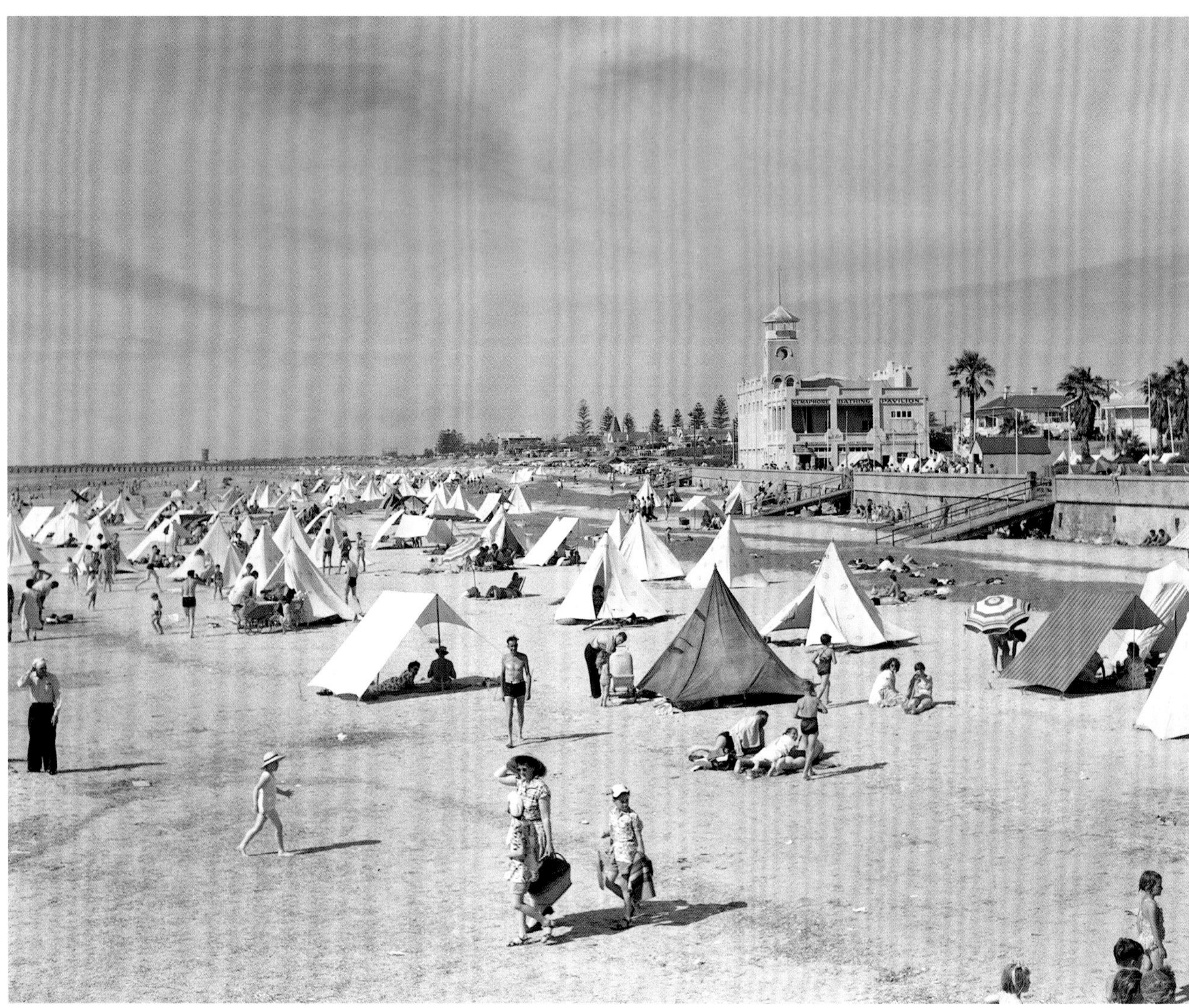

Above: Semaphore beach and the Palais, 1950. The seawall is now completely covered with sand. Opposite: Sandcastle Competition, 1950s. Rex in pith helmet on the right, with George's nephew Laurence and niece Lesley.

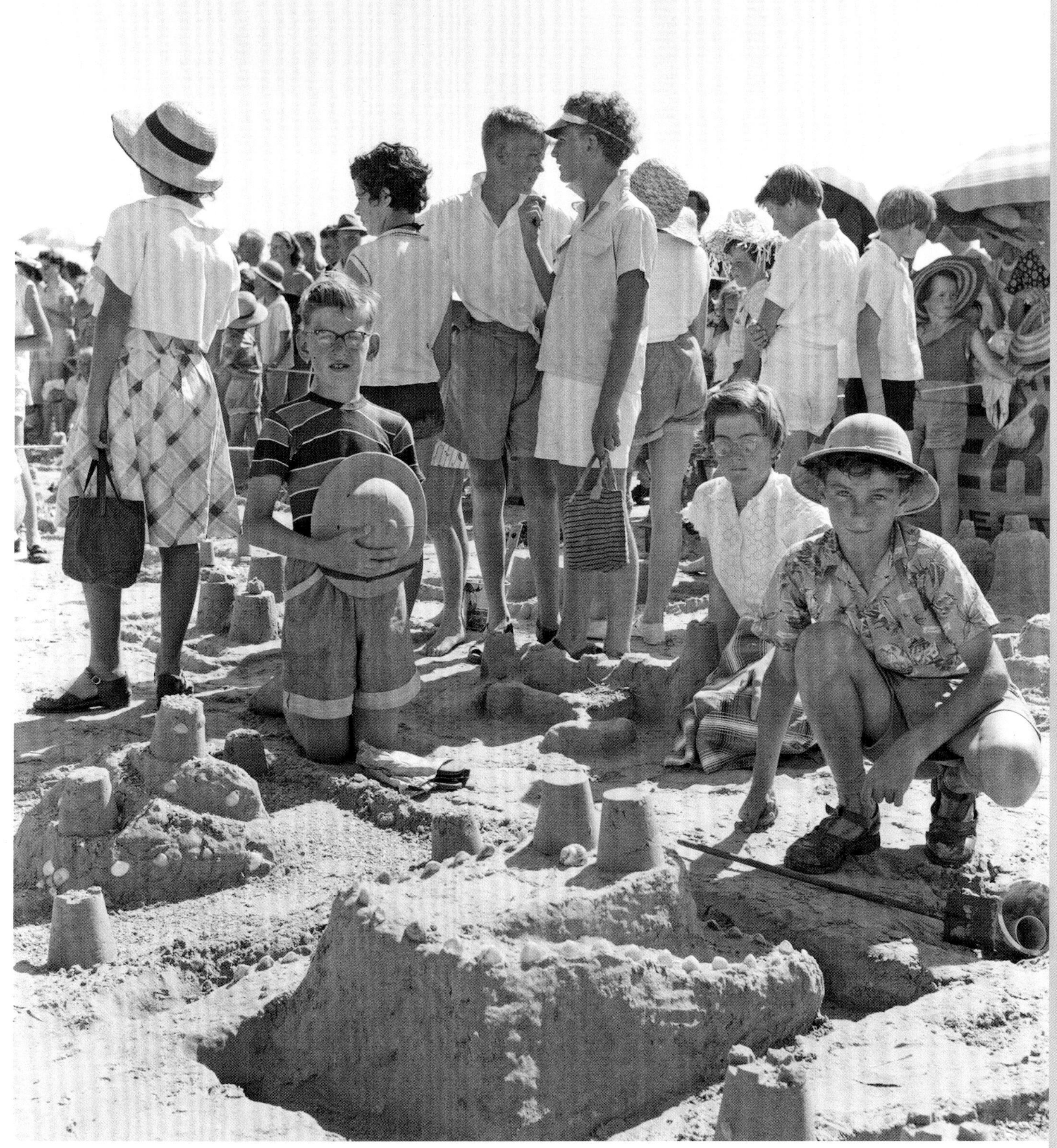

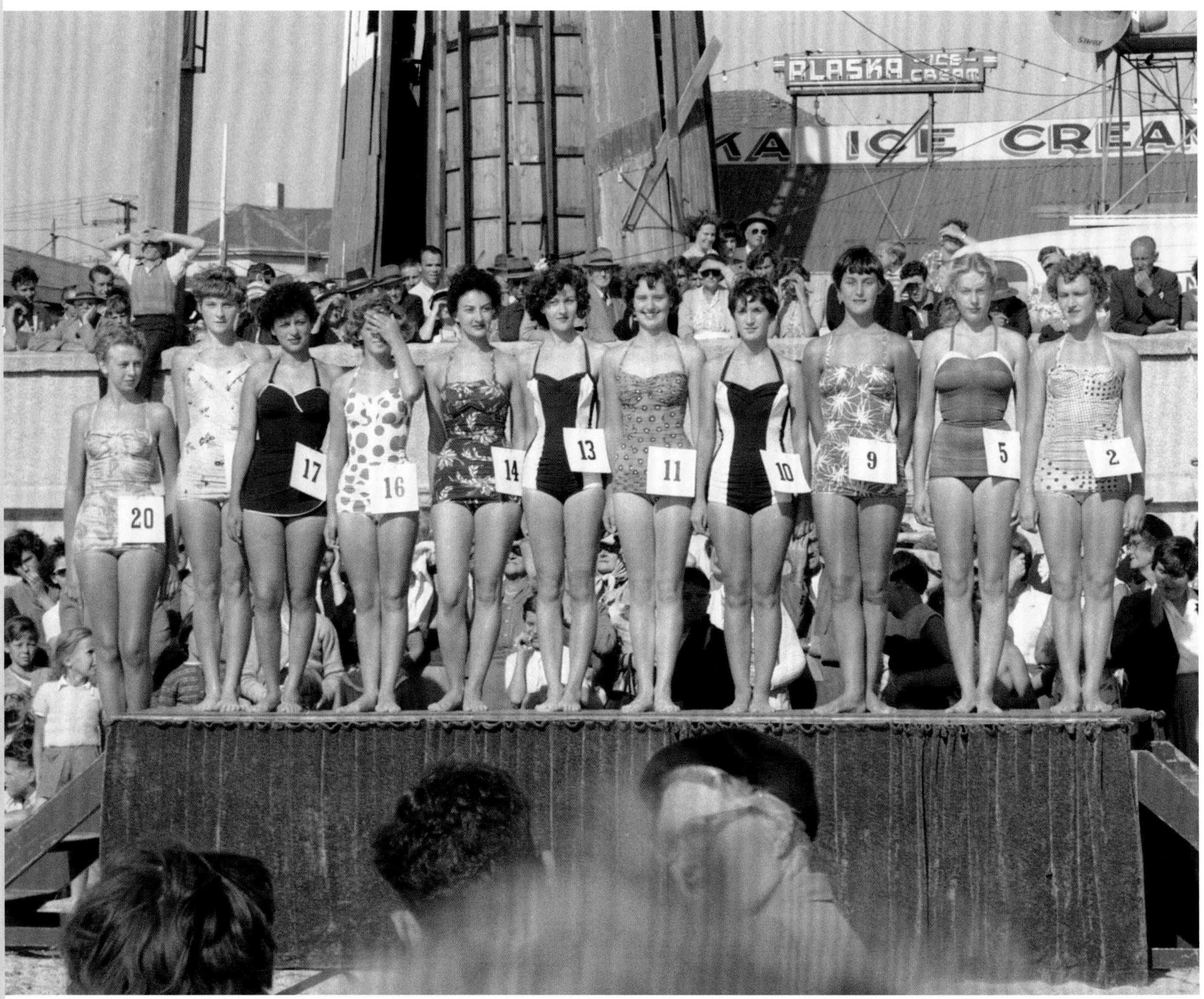

Above: Semaphore Beach Girl, 1950s. Bathing beauty competitions were popular from the 1930s to the 1970s. George was always happy to be the official photographer.

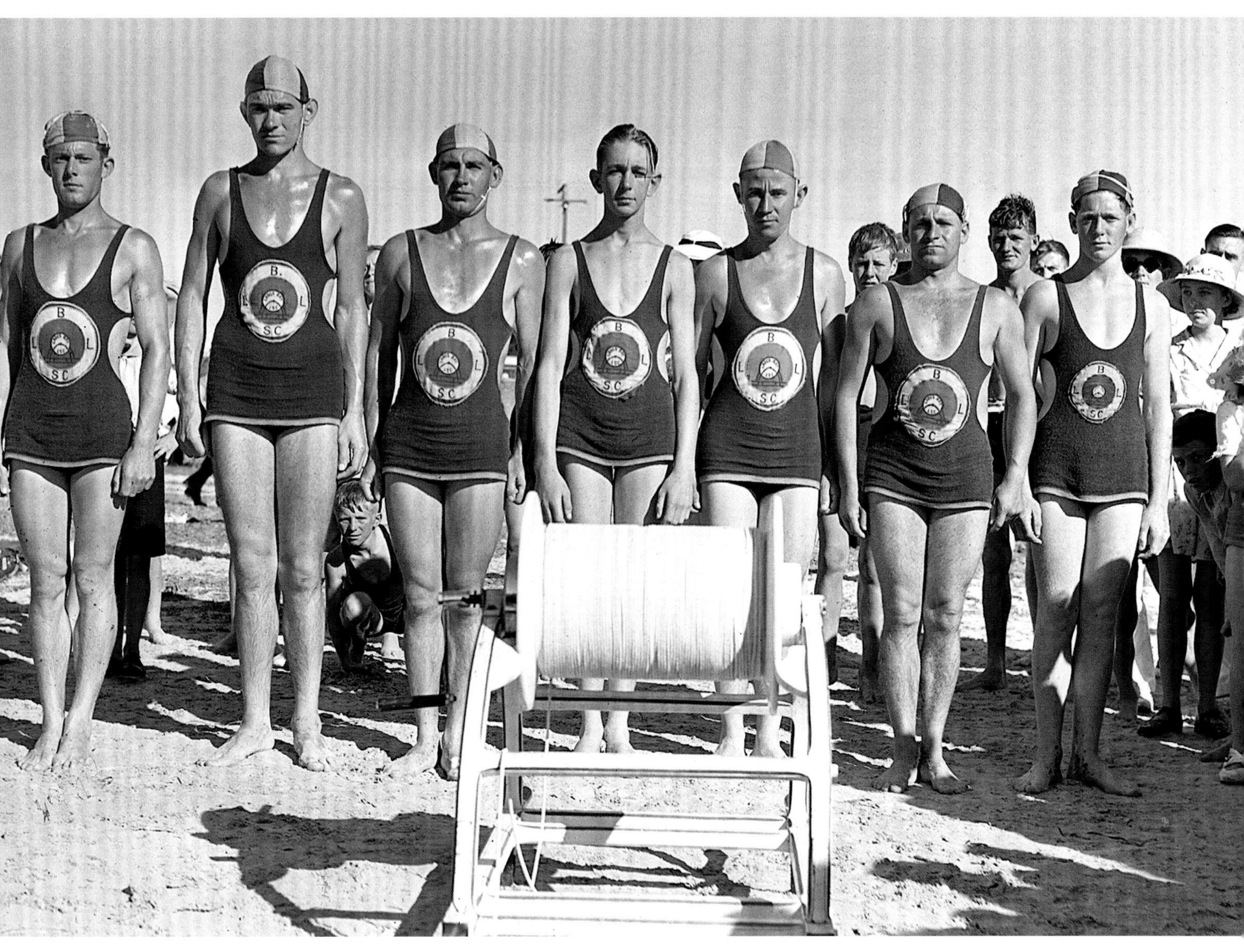

Above: Members of Largs Bay Surf Life Saving Club, sporting their form-fitting woollen bathers, 1950s.

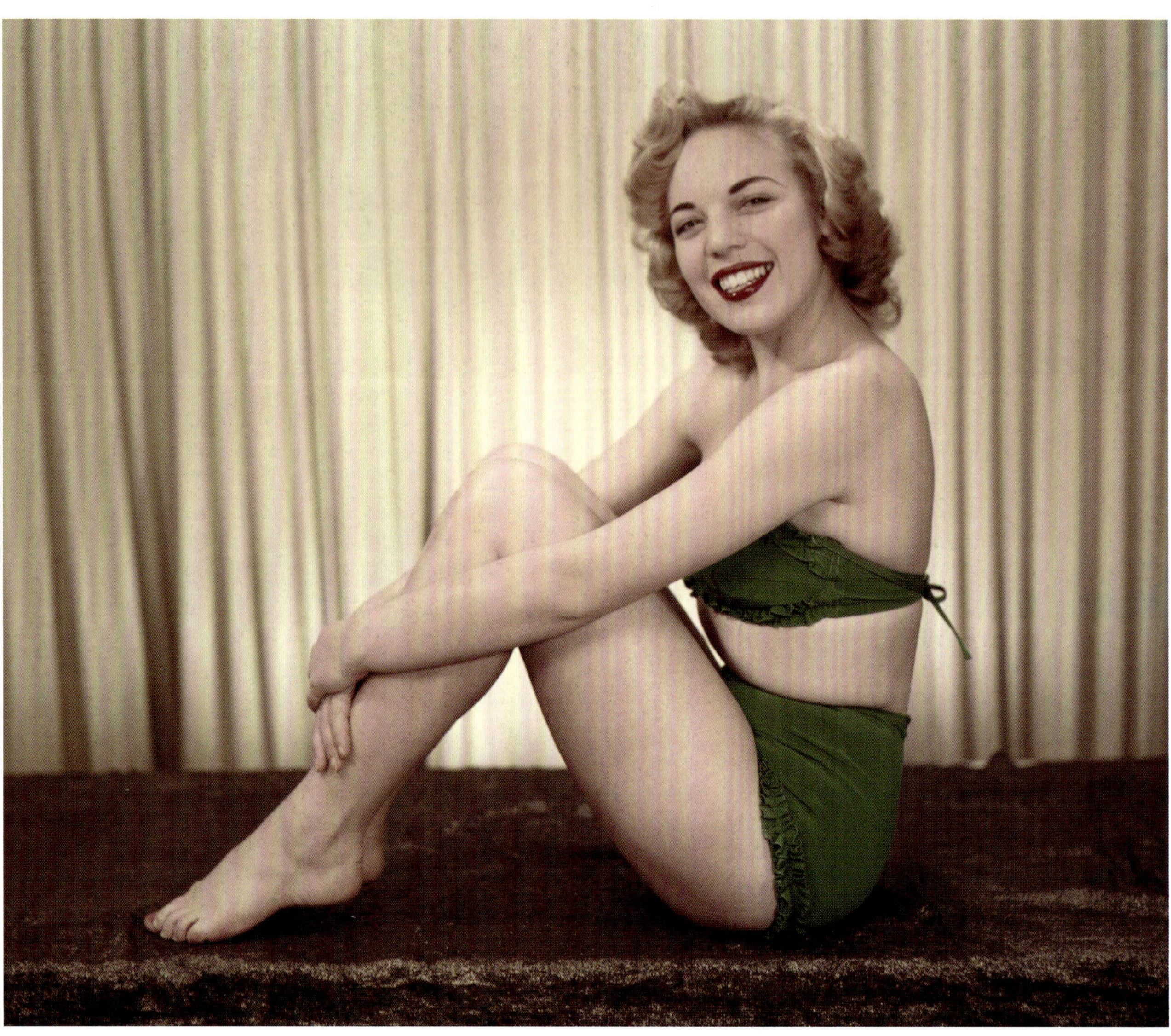

Above: Unknown Marilyn Monroe look-alike model. Studio, 1950s. George photographed aspiring models, who needed professional photographs for their portfolios.

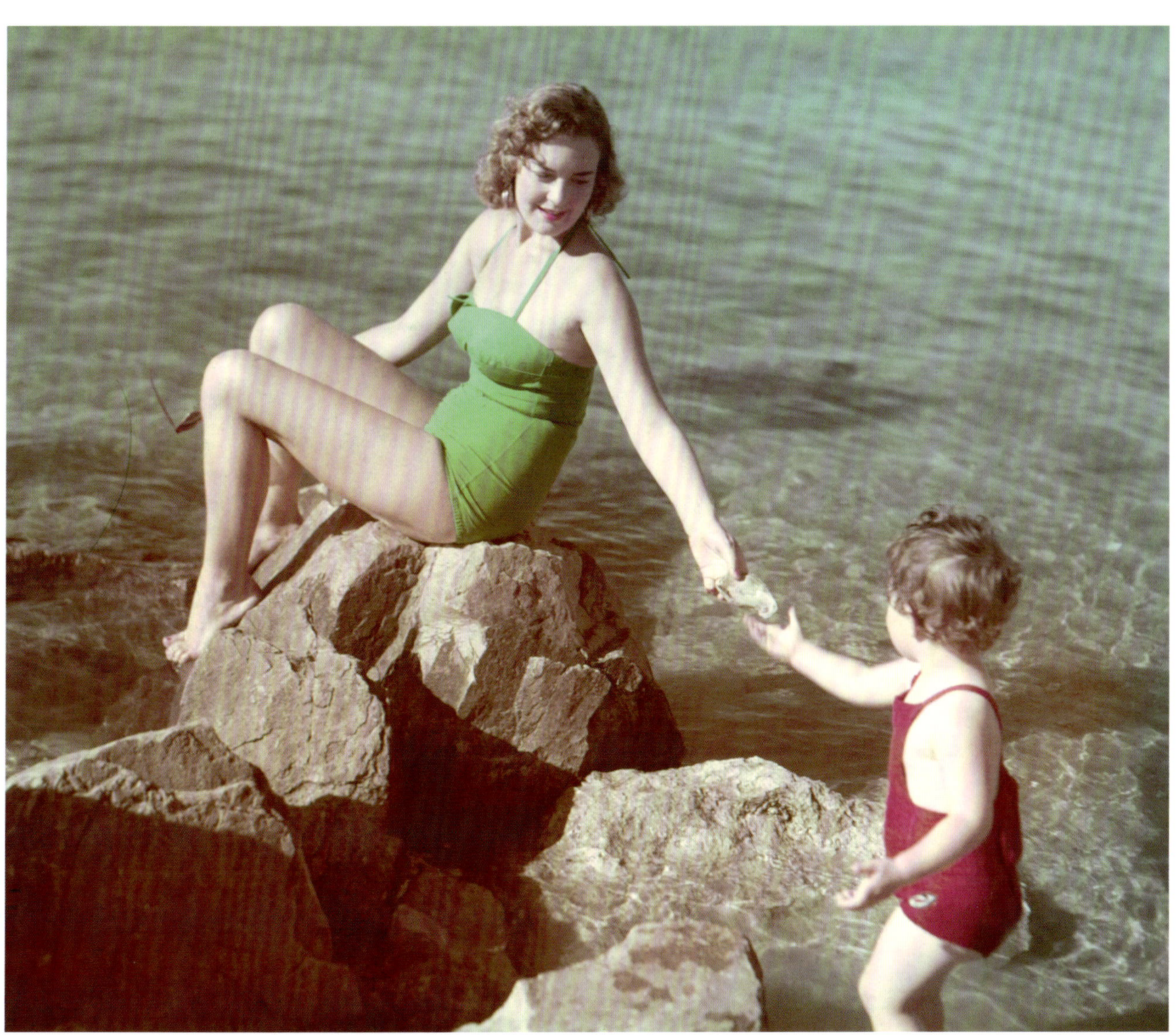

Above: Unknown model. George's daughter acted as a prop on a photoshoot in 1957.

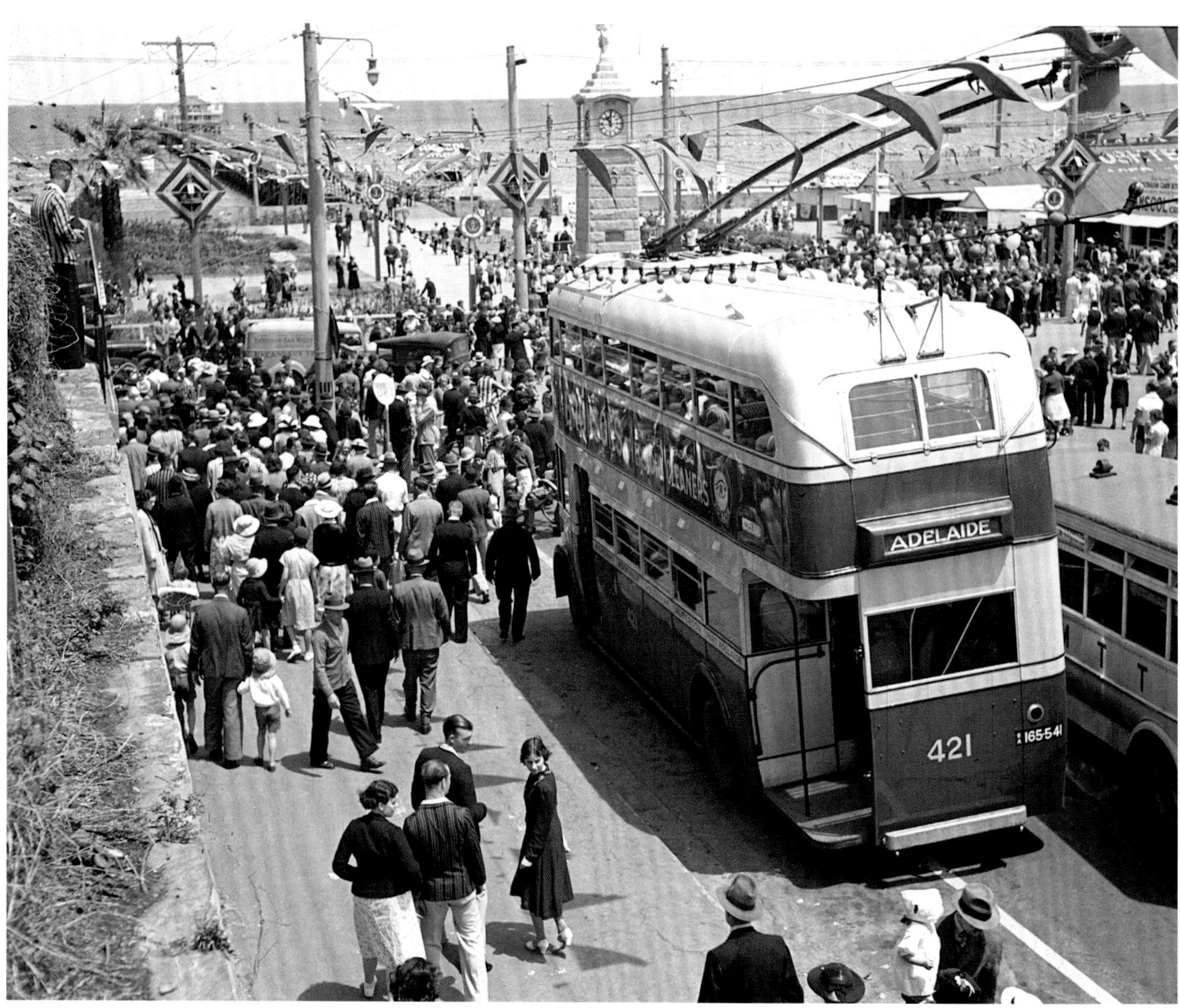

Above: Trolley bus, Semaphore Road and Esplanade, 1940s.

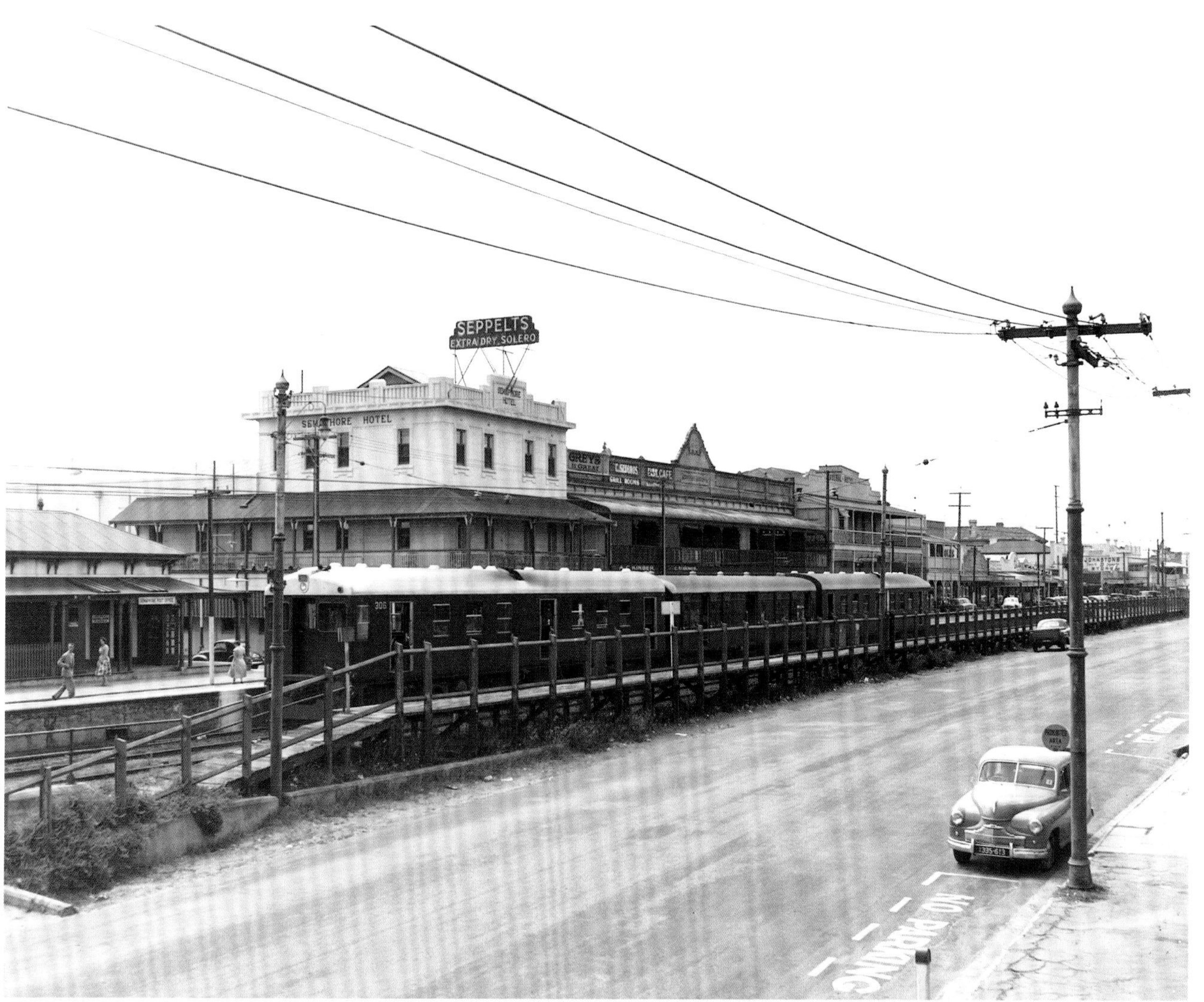

Above: Semaphore Road Red Hen train, 1950s.

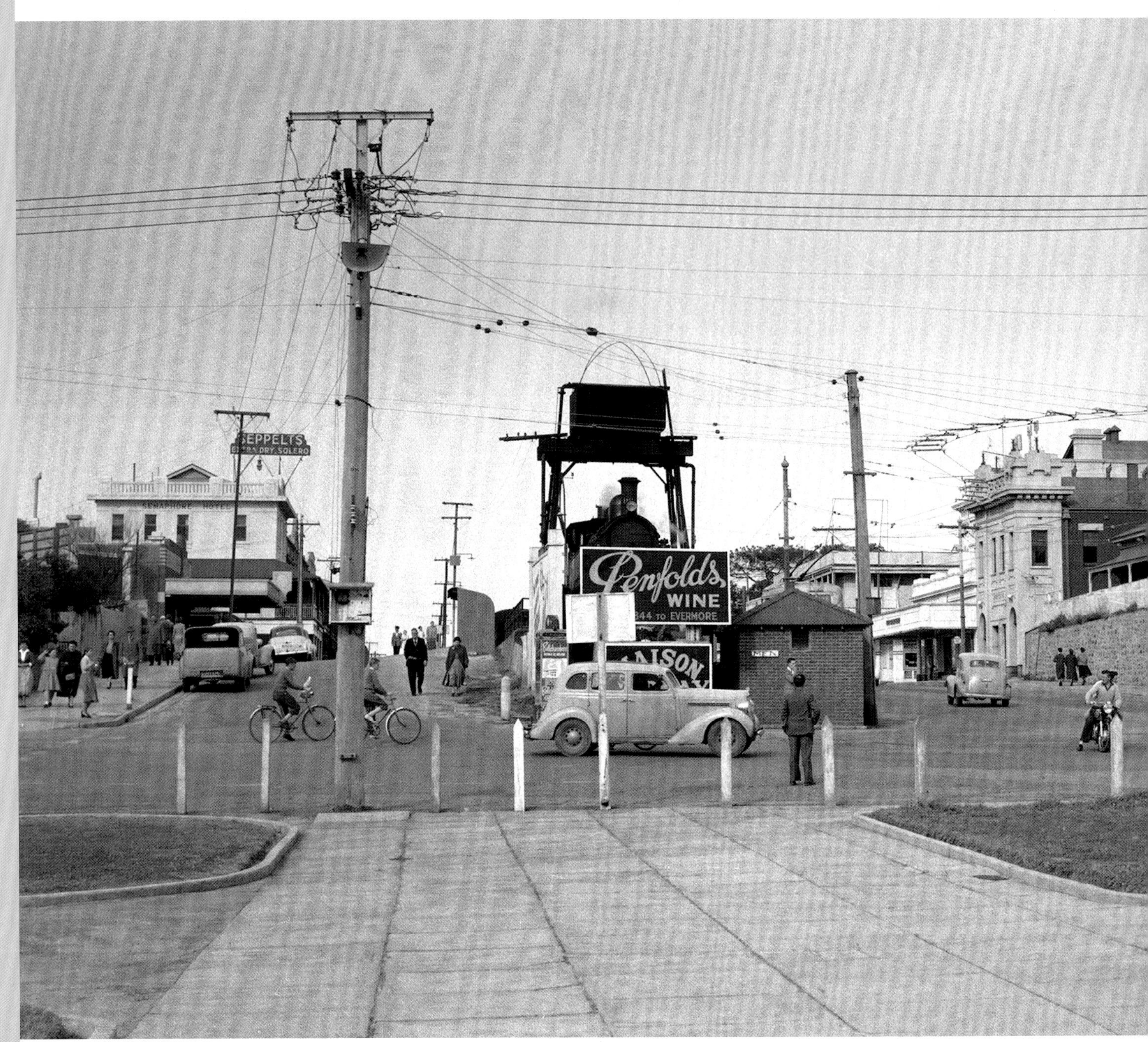

Above: Semaphore Road and Esplanade steam train at station, 1950s.

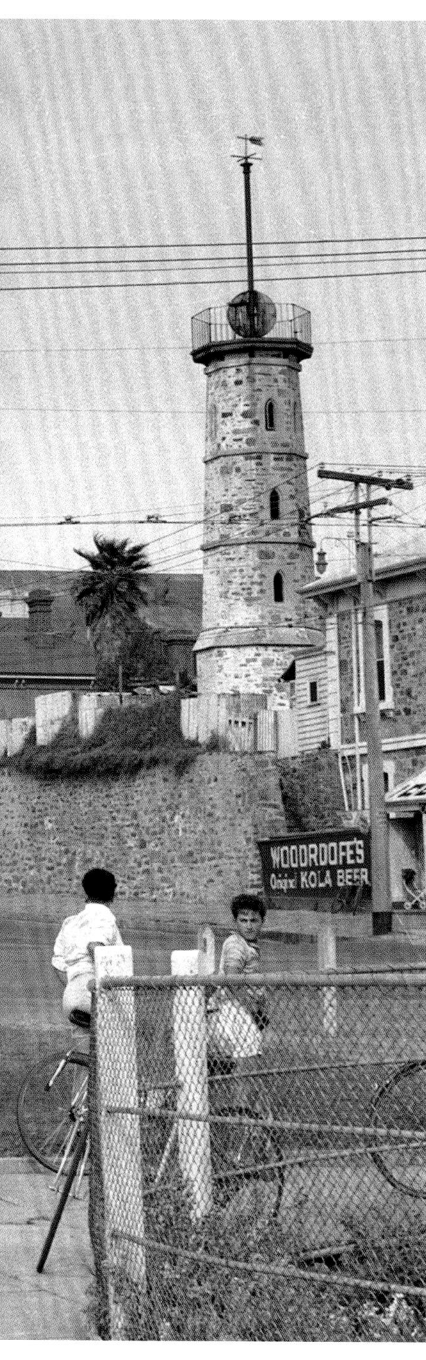

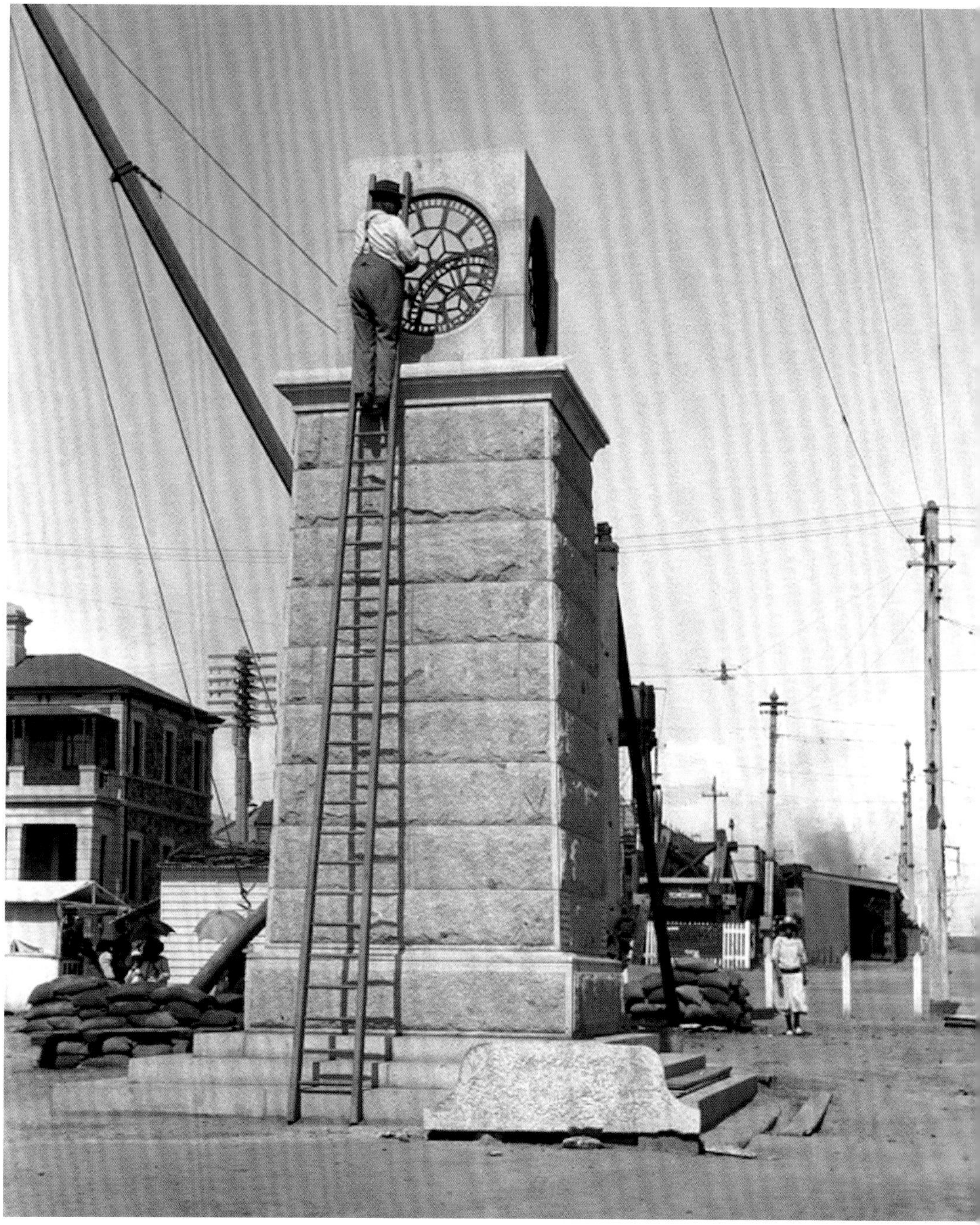

Above: Semaphore Soldiers' Memorial Clock, Harry Topham, 1925.

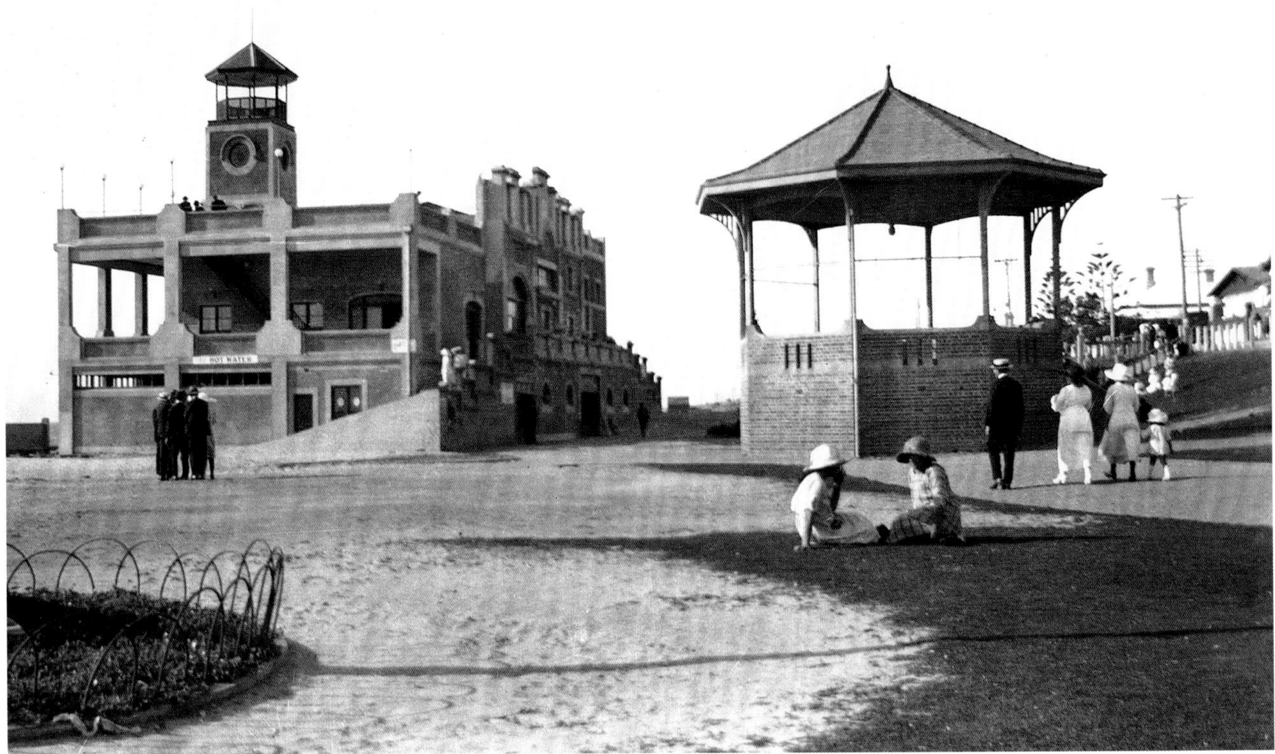

Above: Semaphore Esplanade,
Palais and rotunda, 1924.

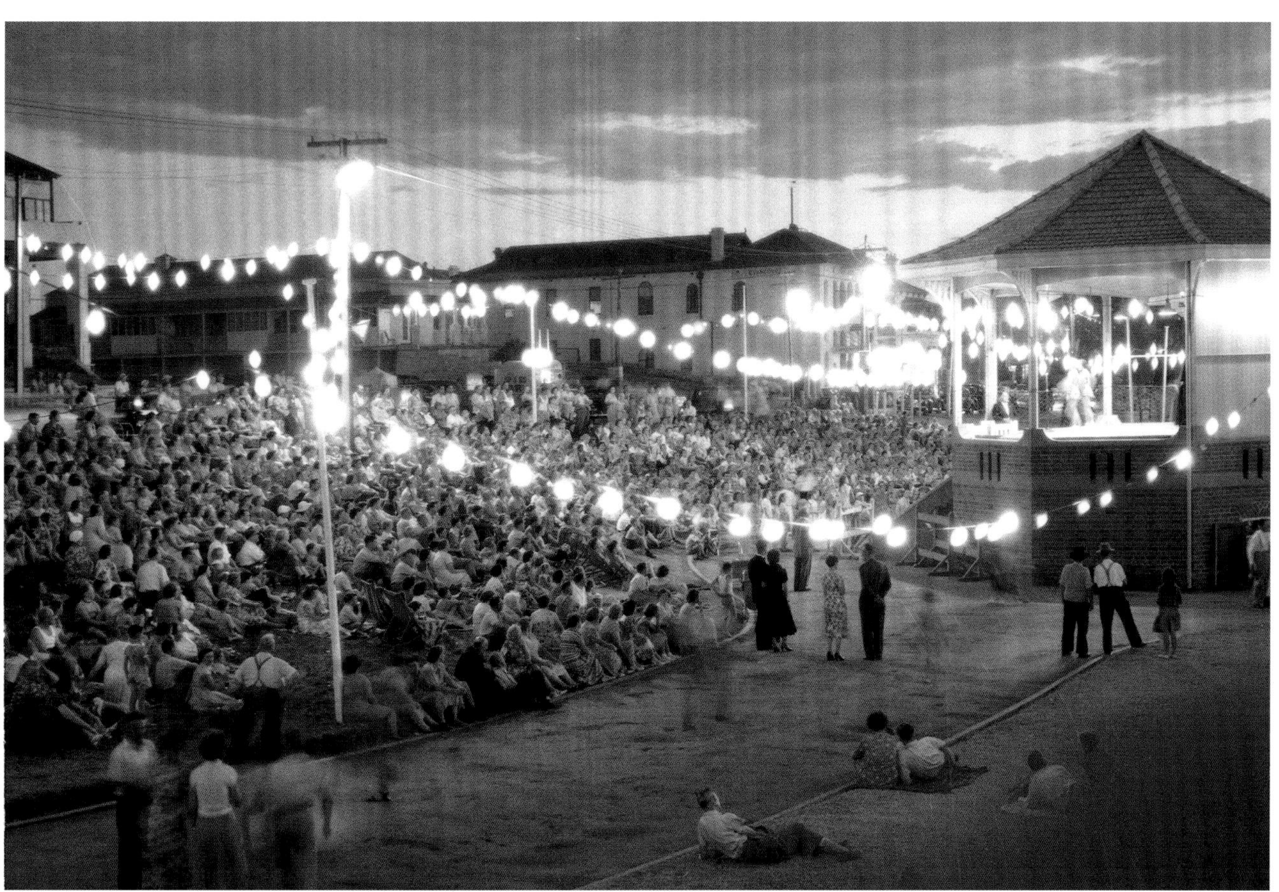

Above: Semaphore beachfront summer bandstand concerts, 1950s.

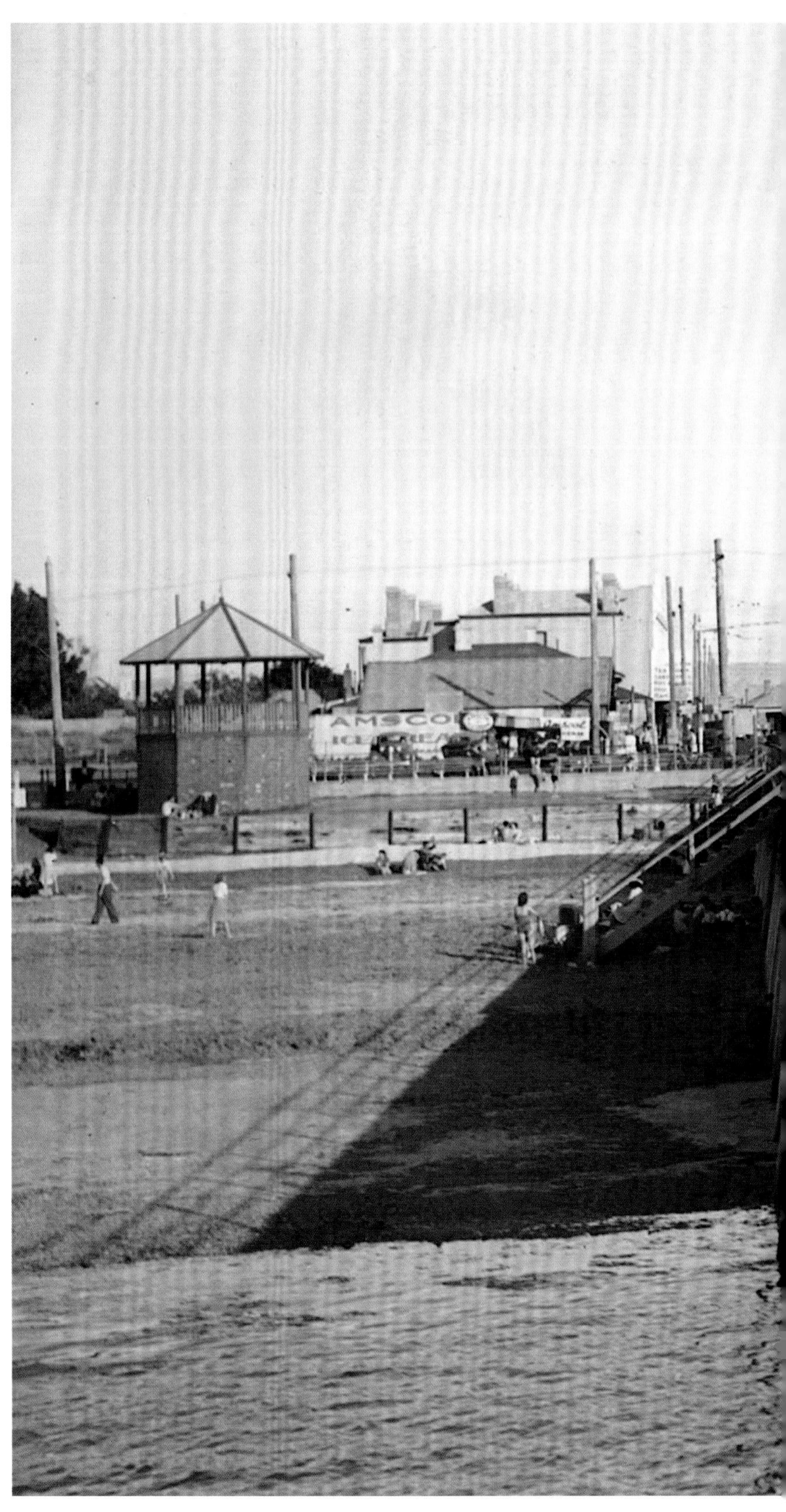

Right: Largs Bay beach, jetty and the Largs Pier Hotel, 1940s.

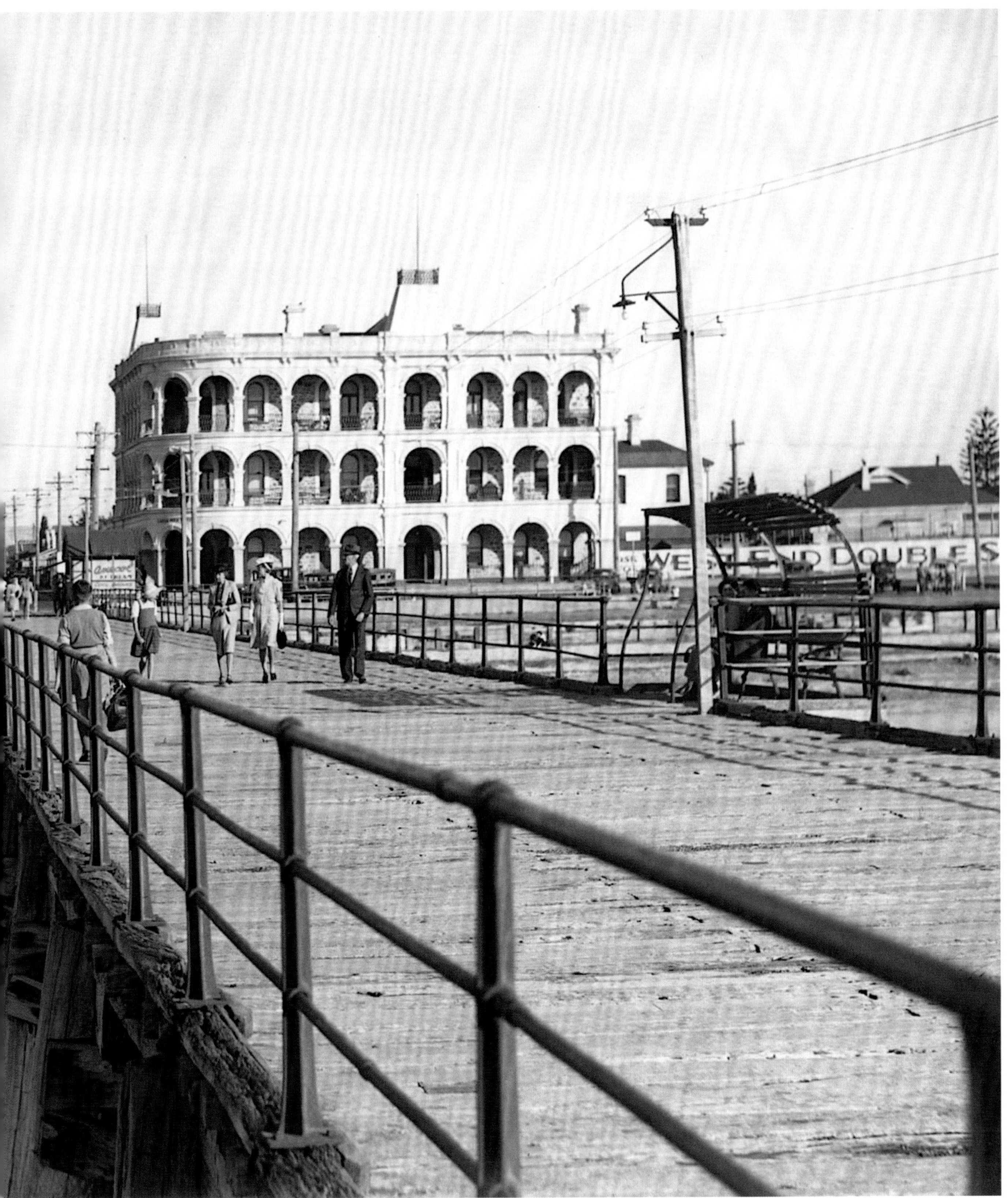
DOUBLES

| EVENTS |

George was always ready with his camera to photograph local events. He would develop, print and display the photos he captured, in the studio showcase window, hoping to attract orders. Not all events were happy ones. George was called out by police in December 1954 to photograph an accident between a train and bus, near Draper station, Largs North. Sadly, several people were killed, and the scene was so distressing that George never spoke of it.

Right: Largs Bay procession, 1950. Clive and Deane Hutton won first prize as a double-headed monster Following spread: Semaphore Road procession, 1954.

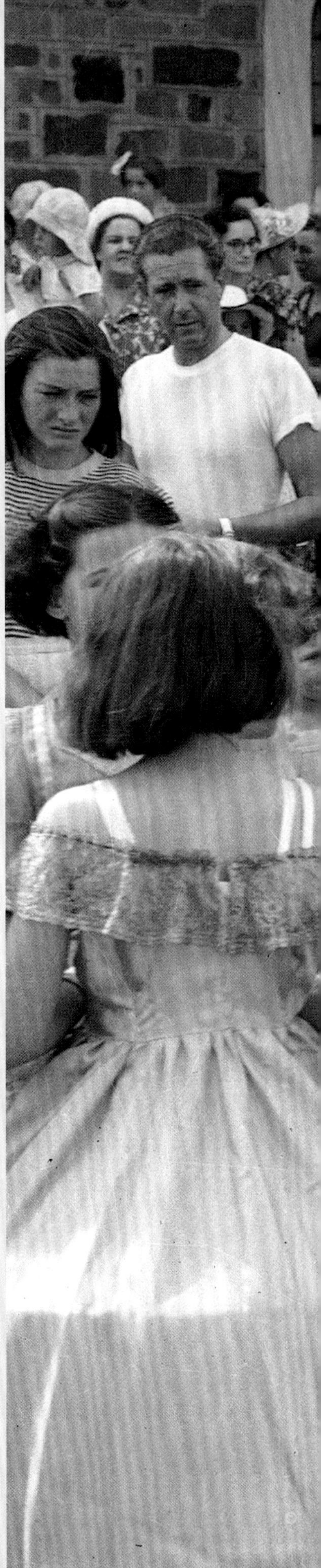

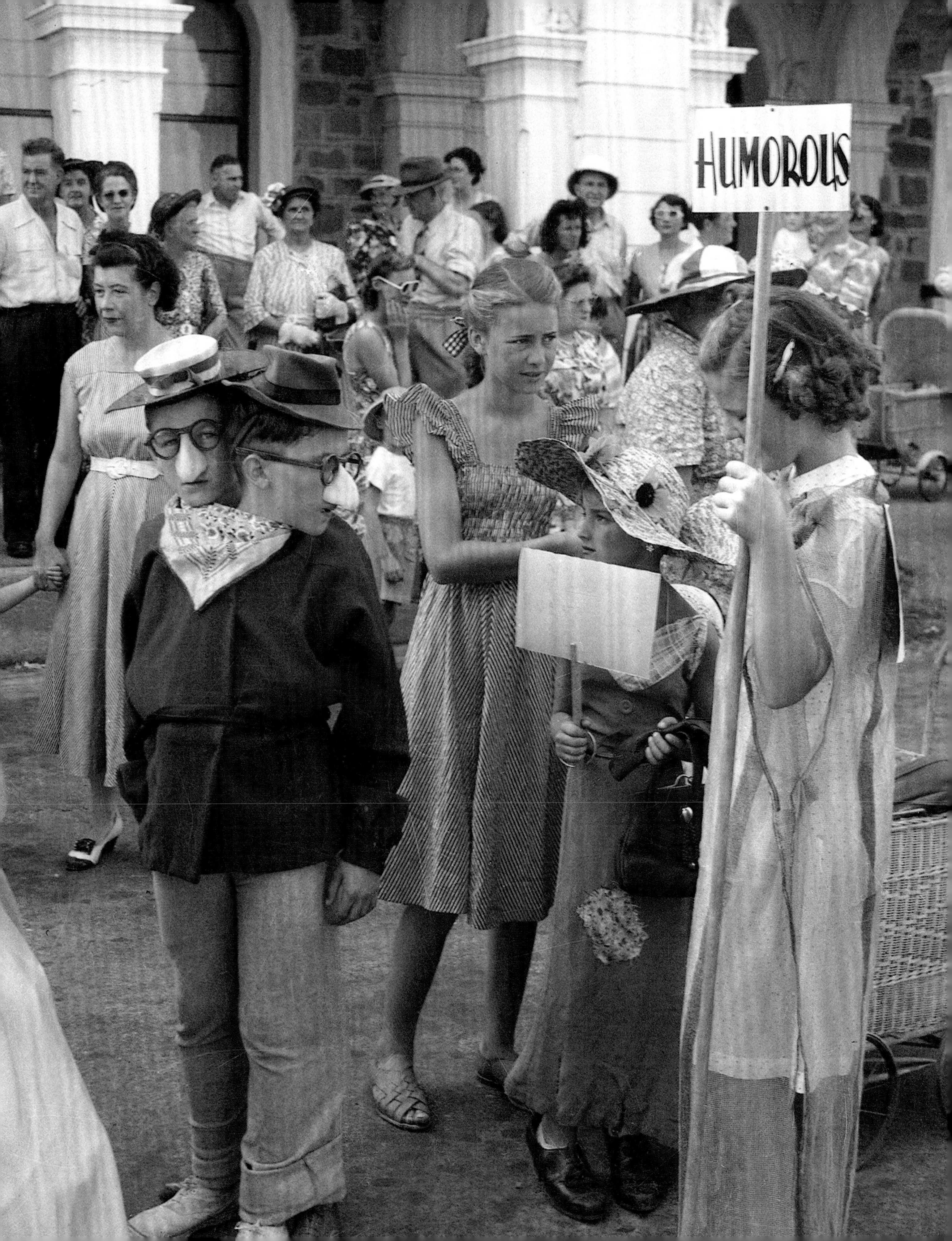
HUMOROUS

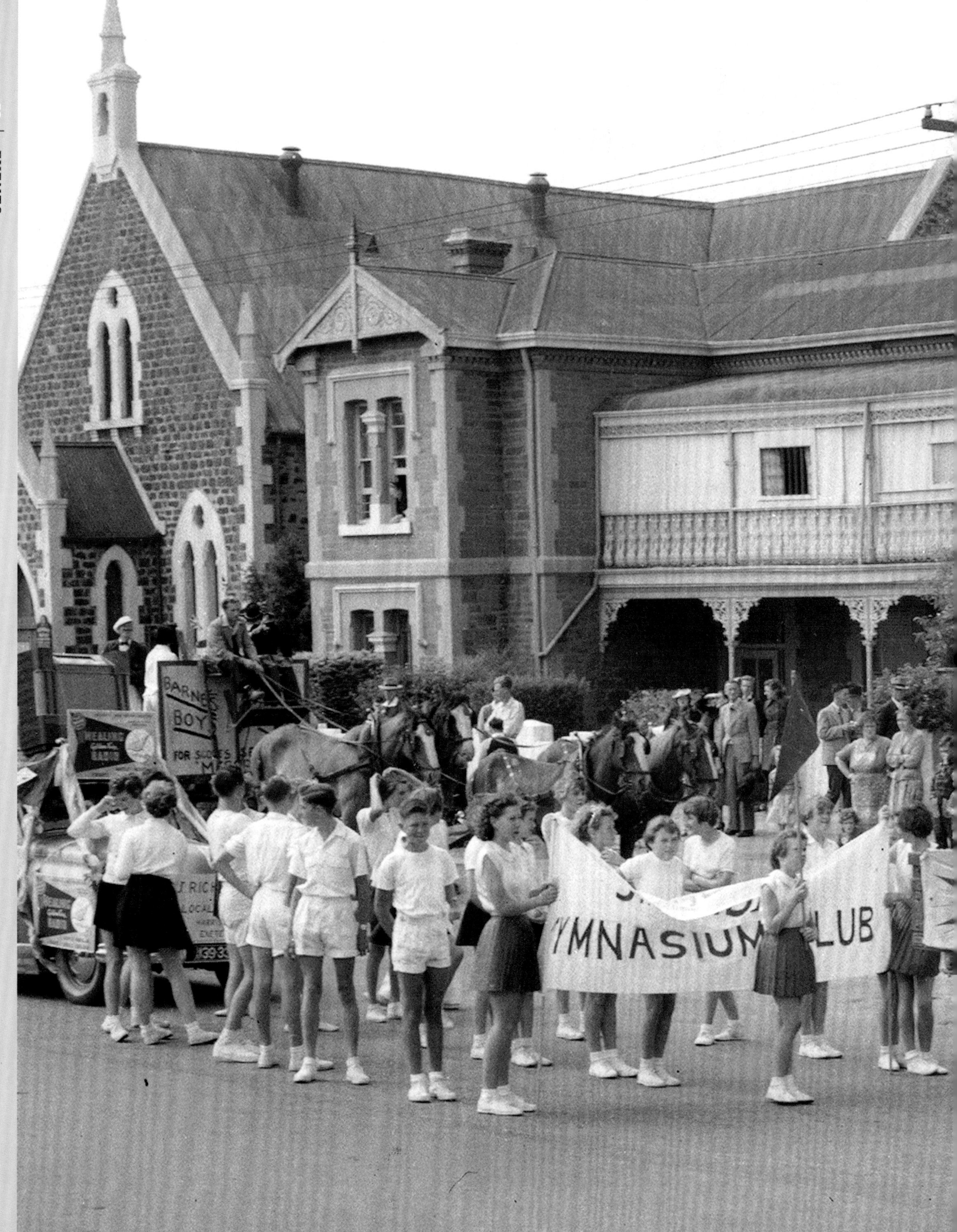
BARNE
BOY
YMNASIUM
LUB

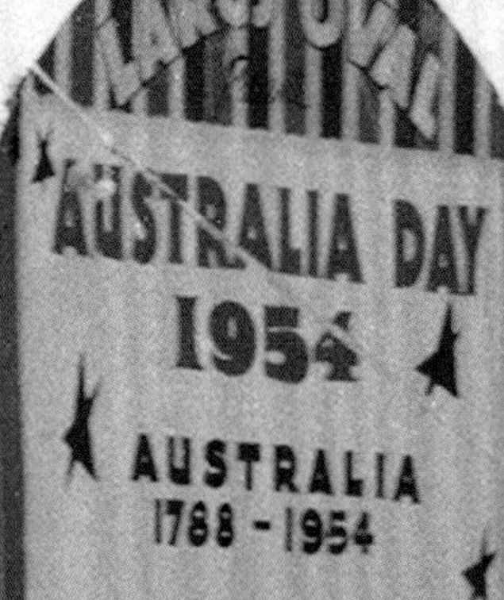
LARGS OVAL
AUSTRALIA DAY
1954
AUSTRALIA
1788 - 1954
CALTEX
NEW
Super Swift
GROCERY
DELIVERY SERVICE
PORT ADELAIDE
MEDINDIE
ROSEWATER
PORT AUGUSTA

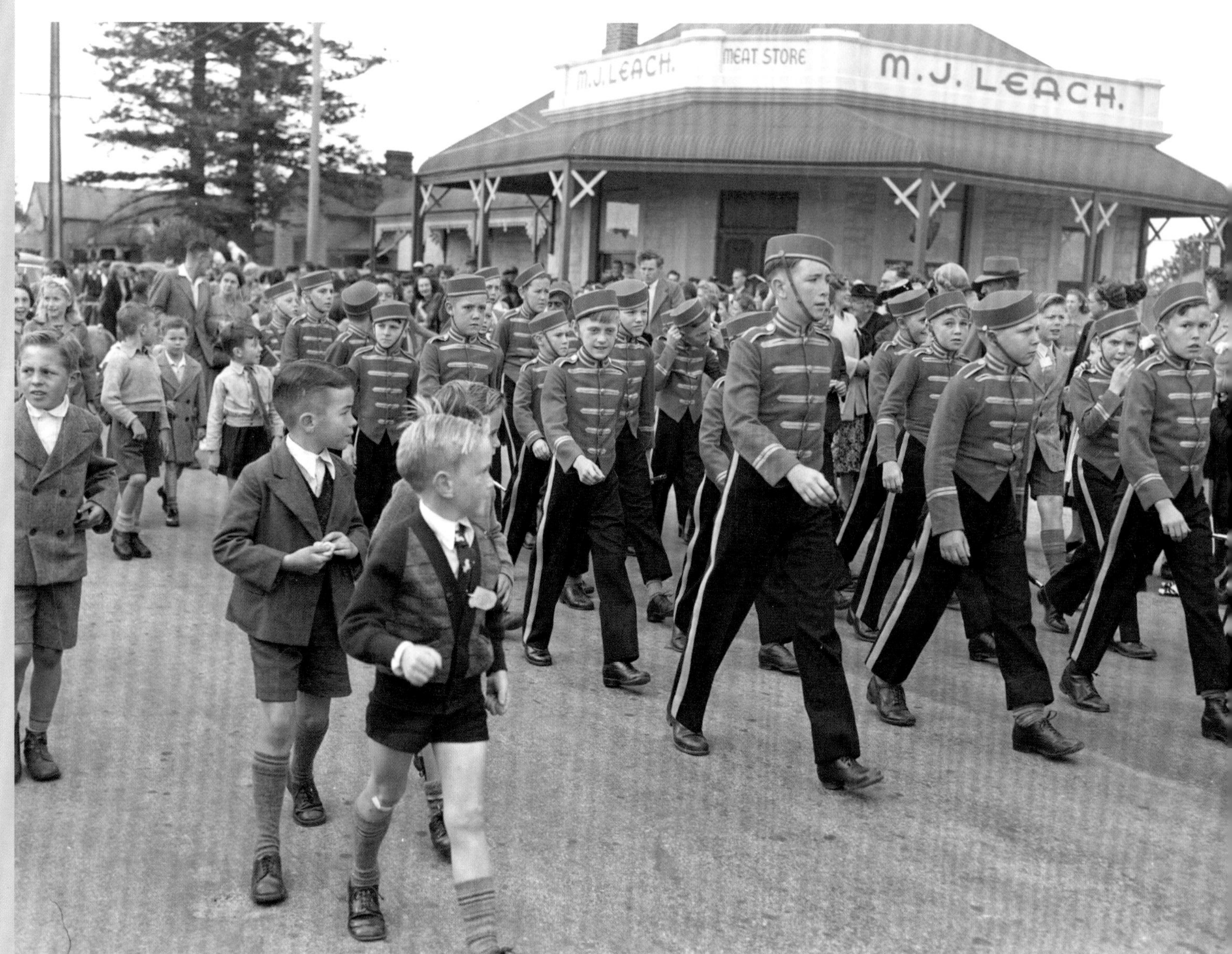

Above: Primary School band, 1940s.

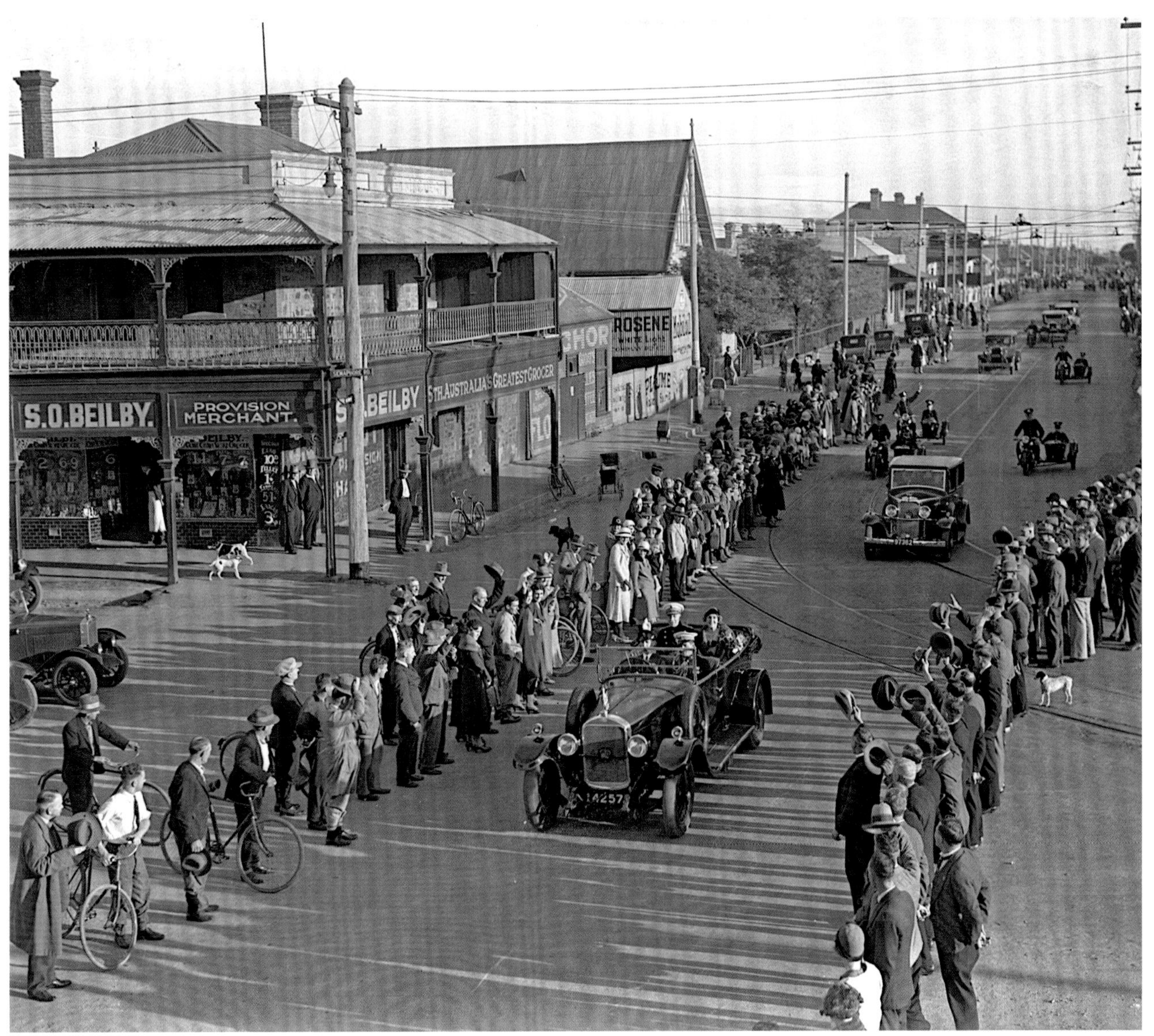

Above: Corner of Semaphore Road and Military Road. Lady Gowrie on her way to open Lady Gowrie Drive, 1936.

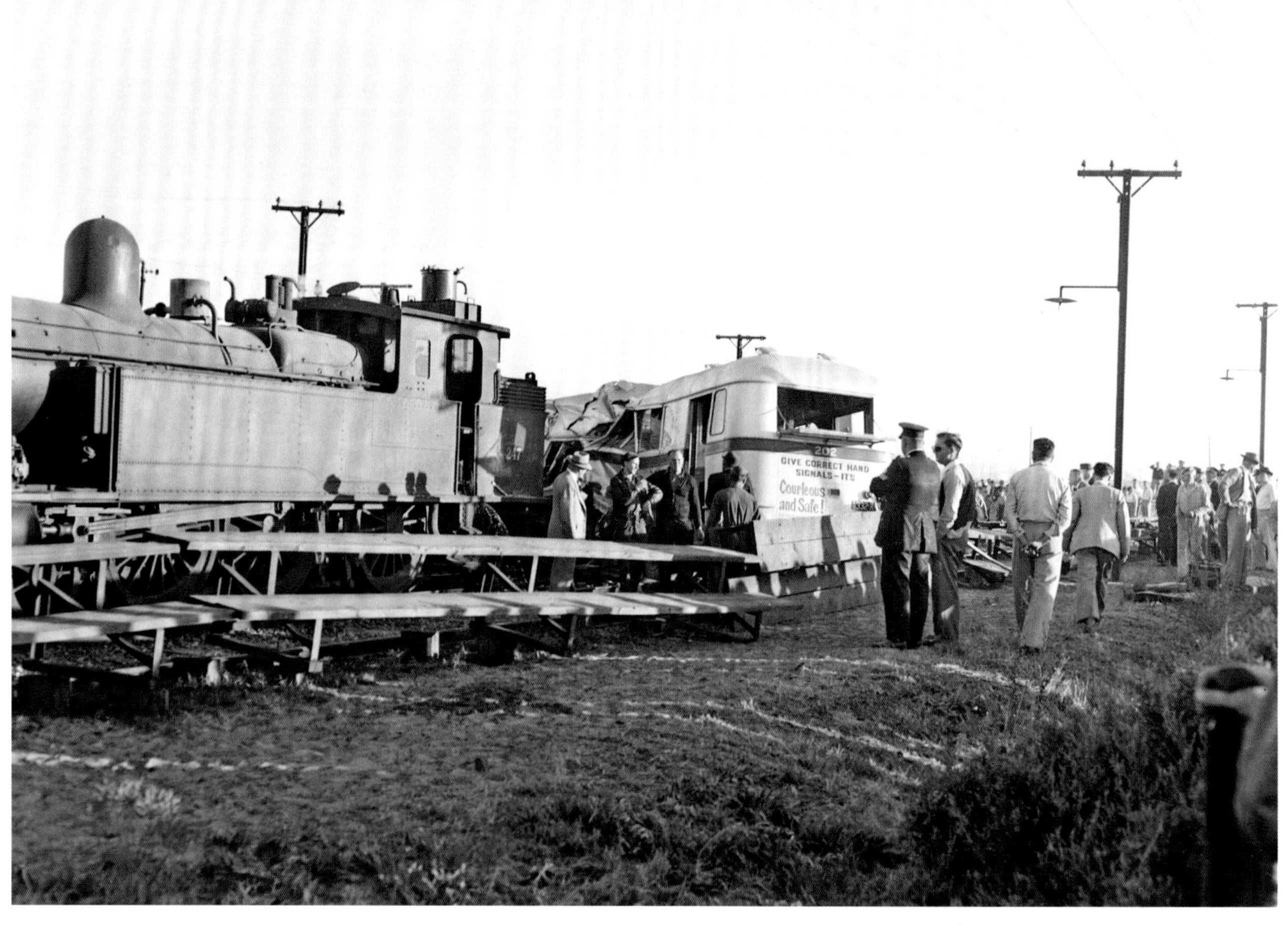

Above: Train and bus crash, Draper level crossing, December 1954.

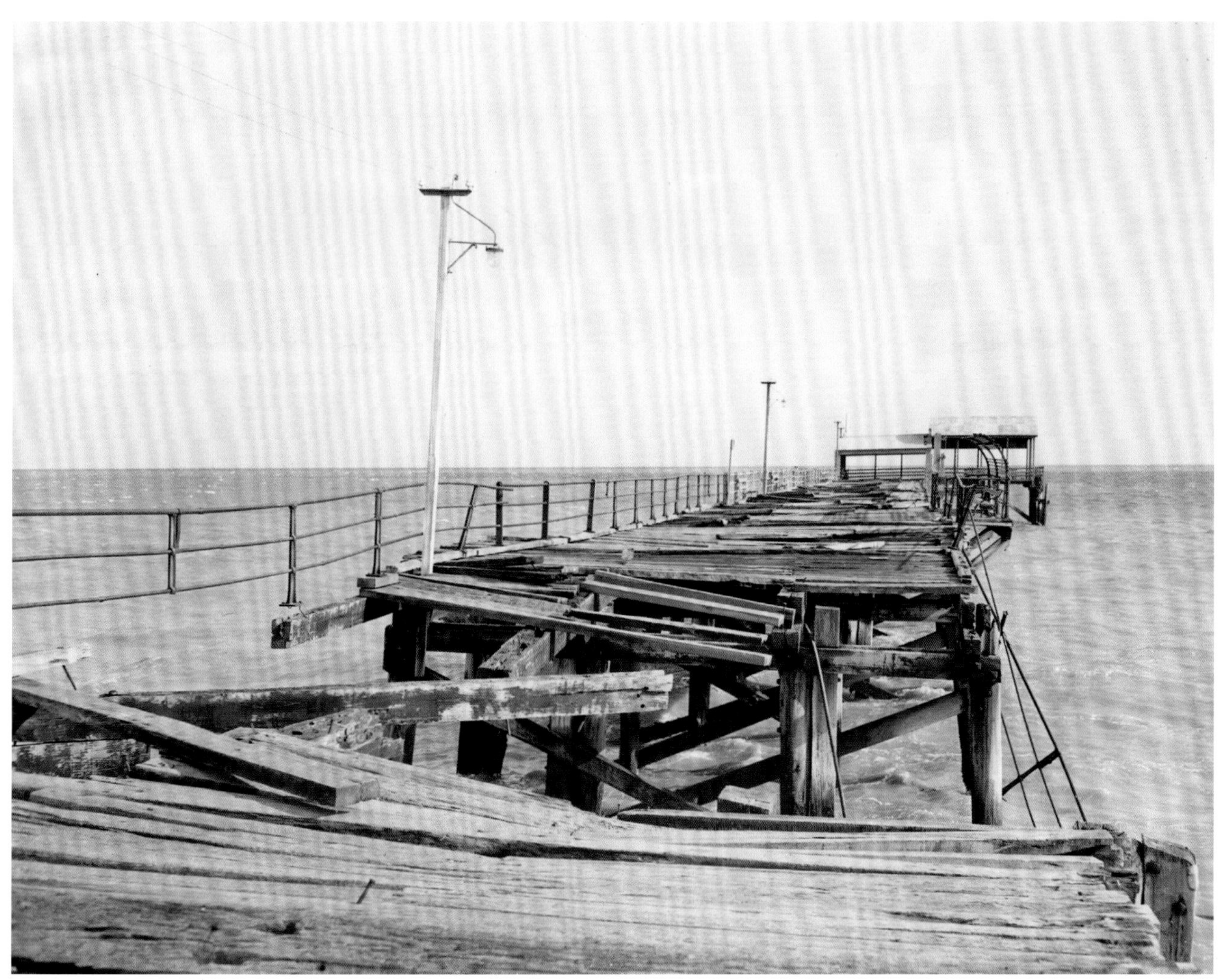

Above: Largs Bay Jetty storm damage, 1953.

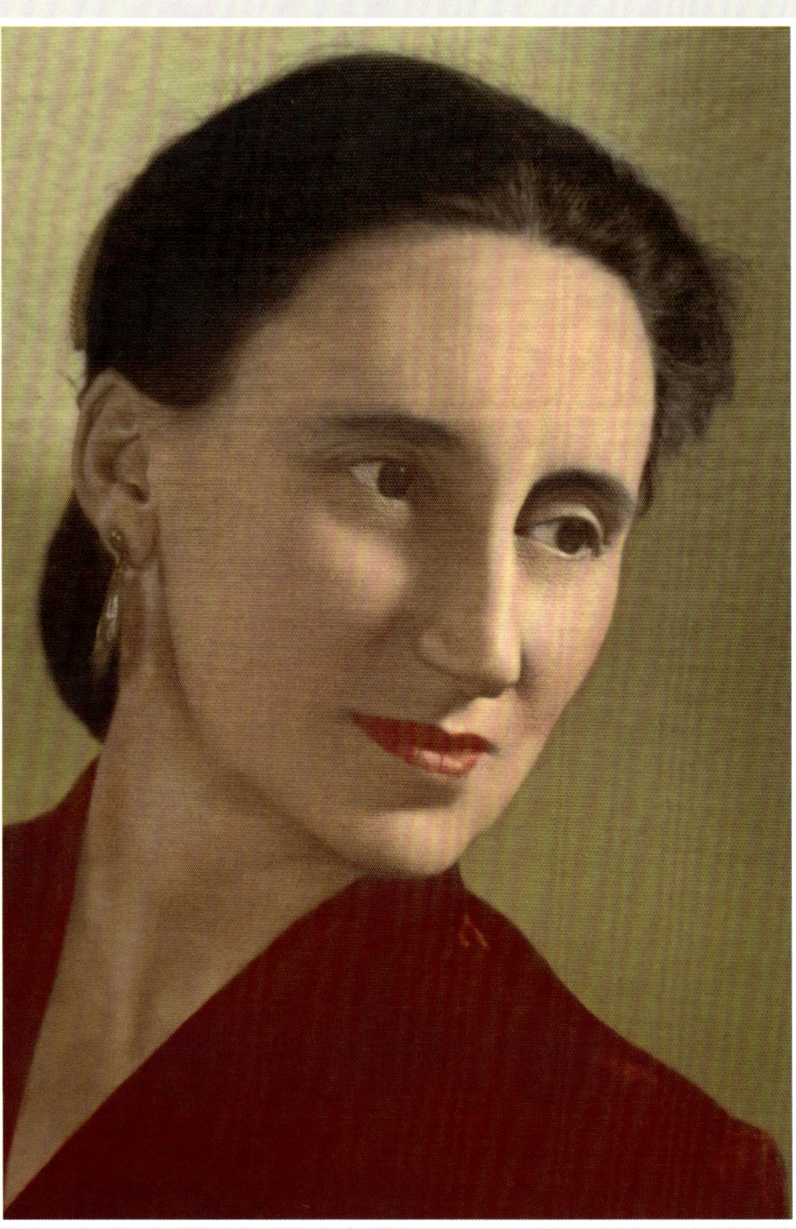

Above: Audrey Hutton, 1954, using Rembrandt lighting.

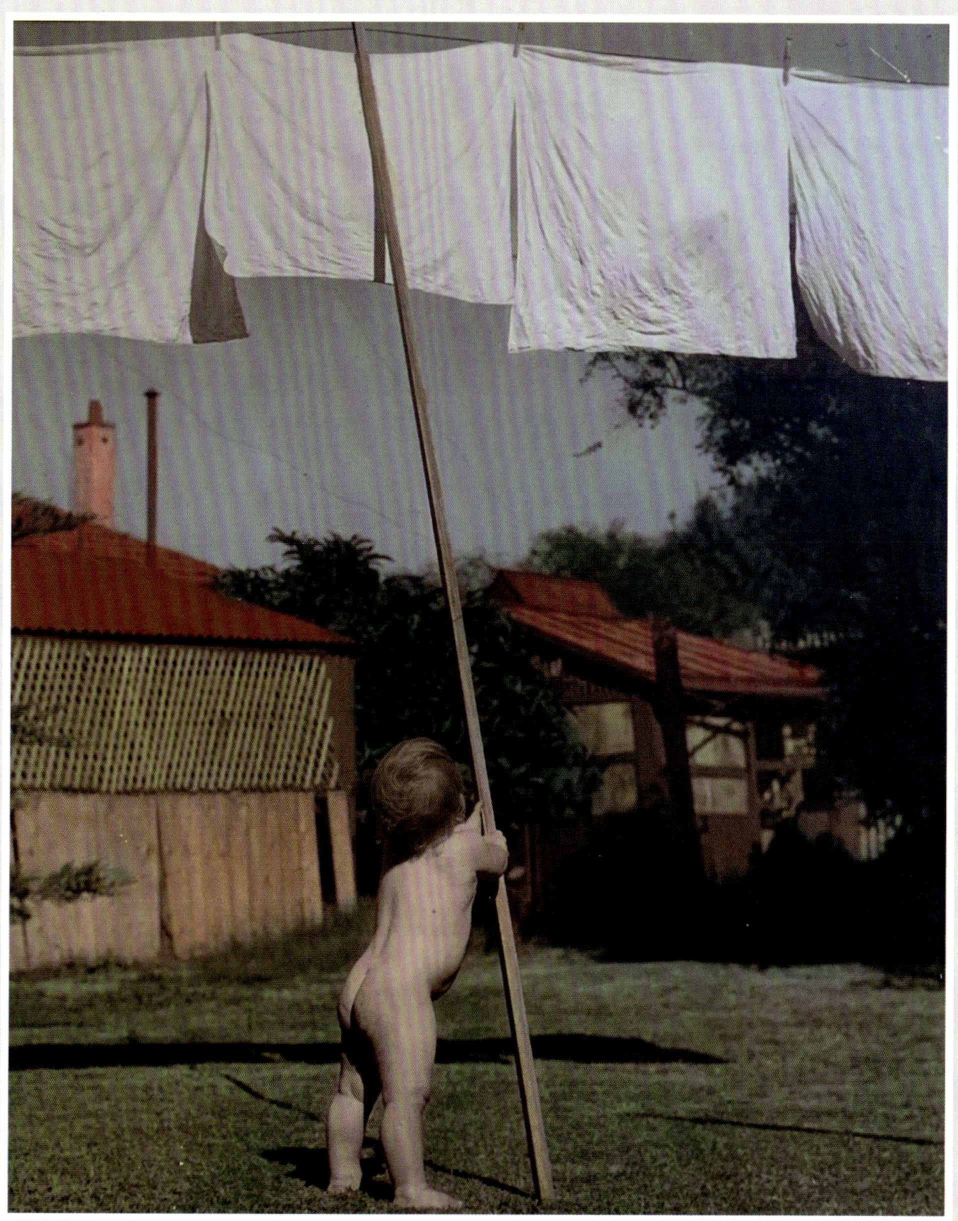

Above: Clive Hutton under washing line, 1941. This was a competition entry, entered in sepia and hand-coloured.

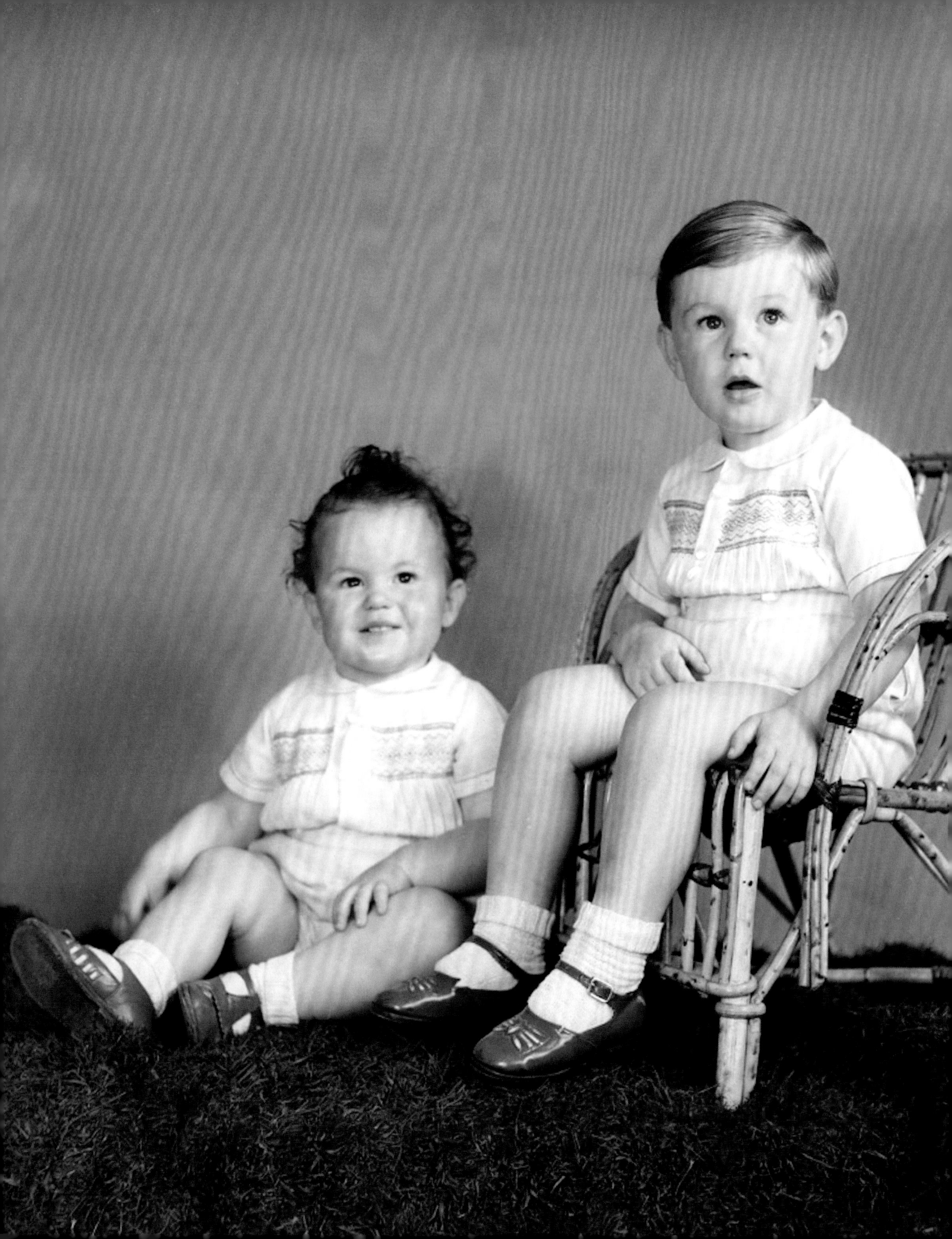

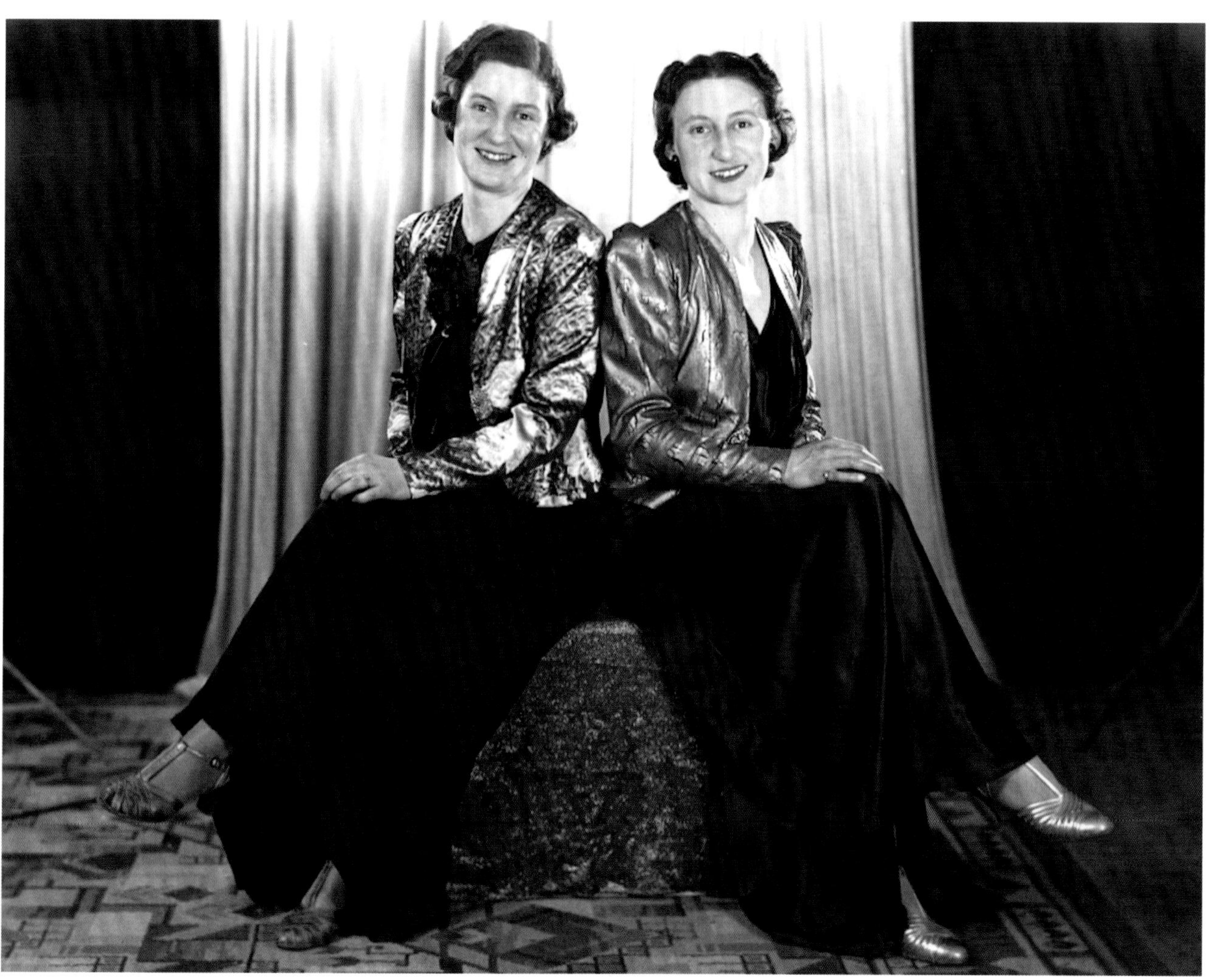

Above: Sisters Audrey Hutton and Laurel Knowles, 1939.
Opposite: Brothers, Clive and Deane Hutton, 1943.

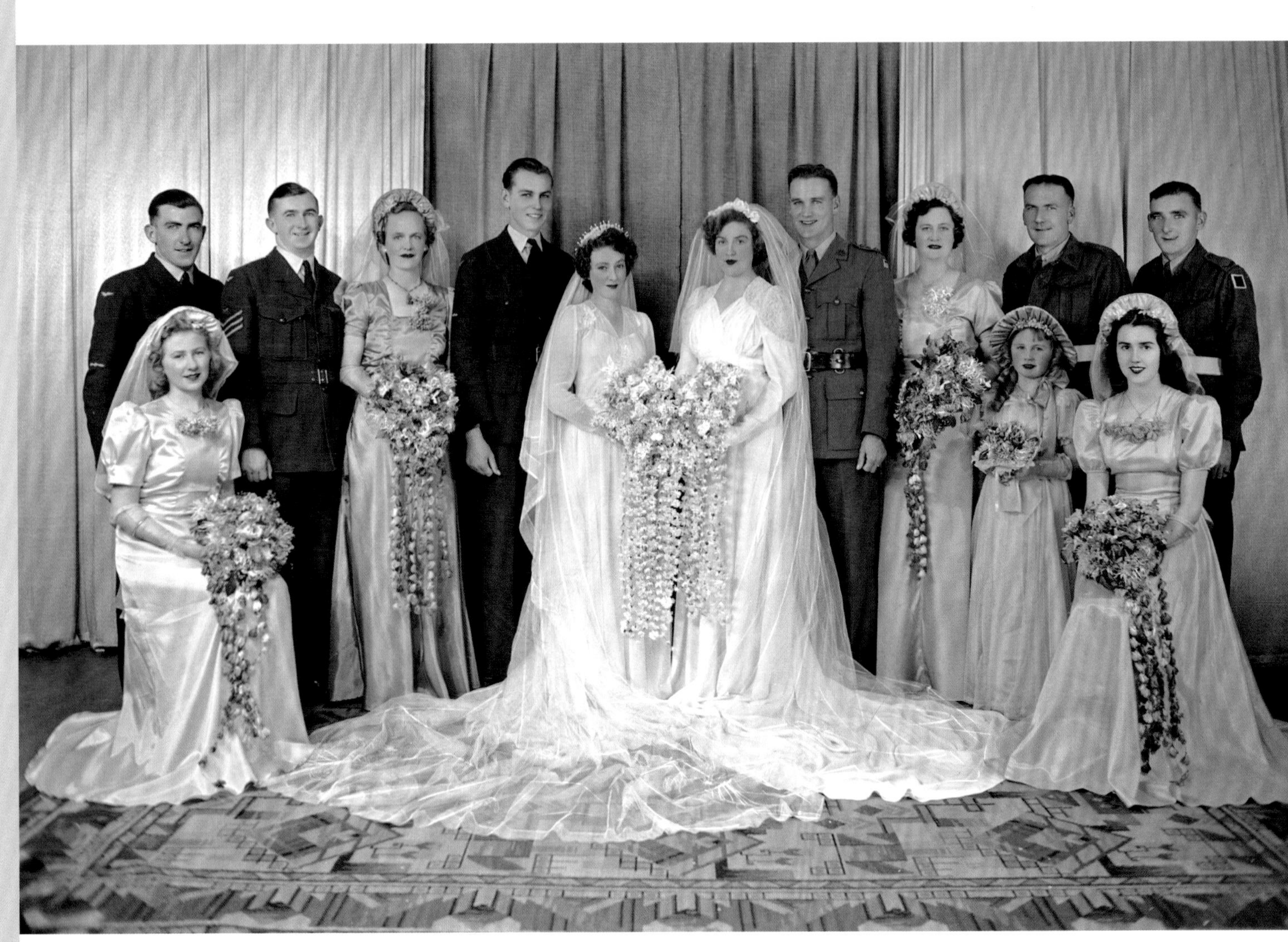

Above: Wartime double wedding, 1943.

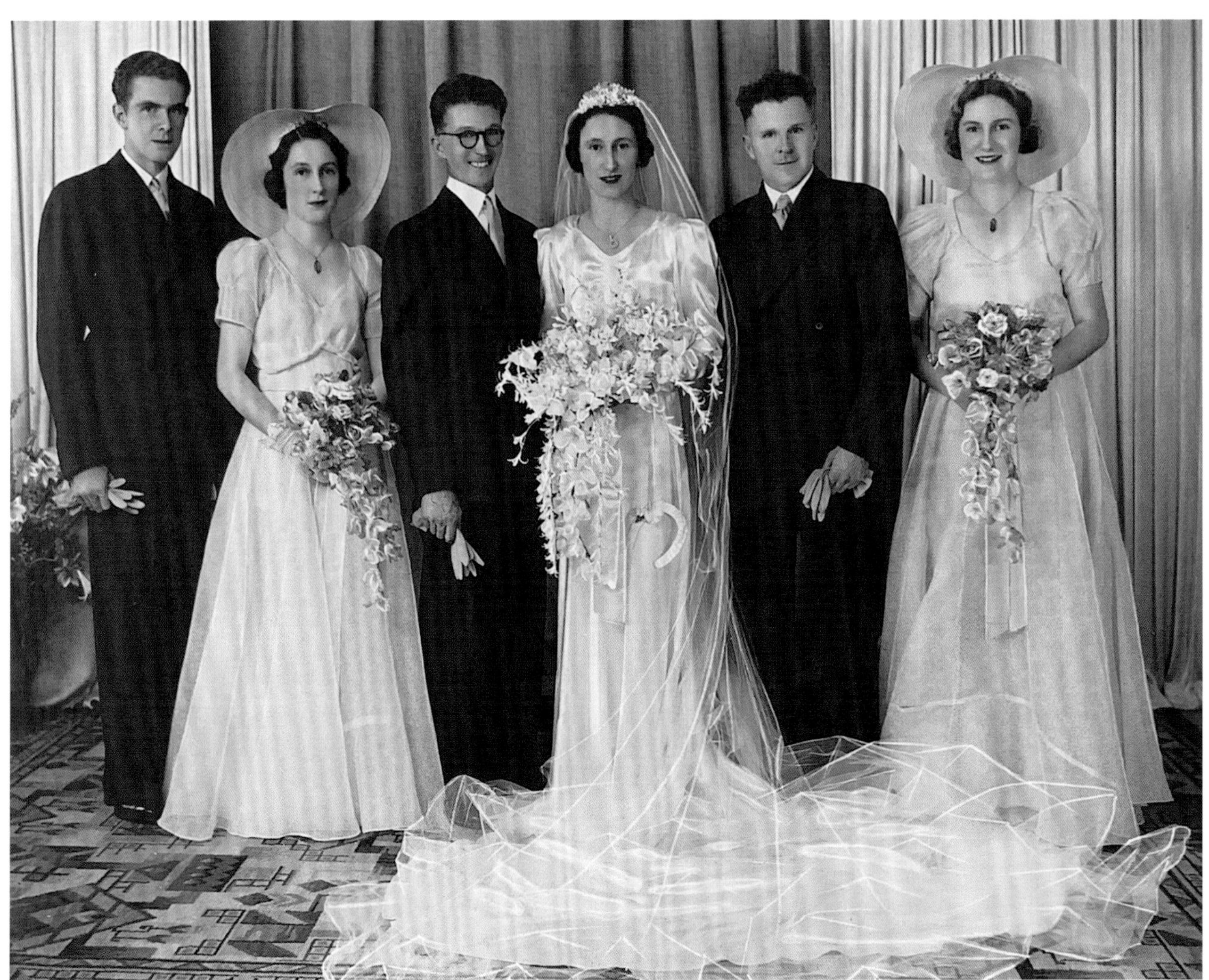

Above: George and Audrey, 1939. L to R: Ron Coudrey, Norma Knowles, George, Audrey, Charlie Hutton, Laurel Knowles.

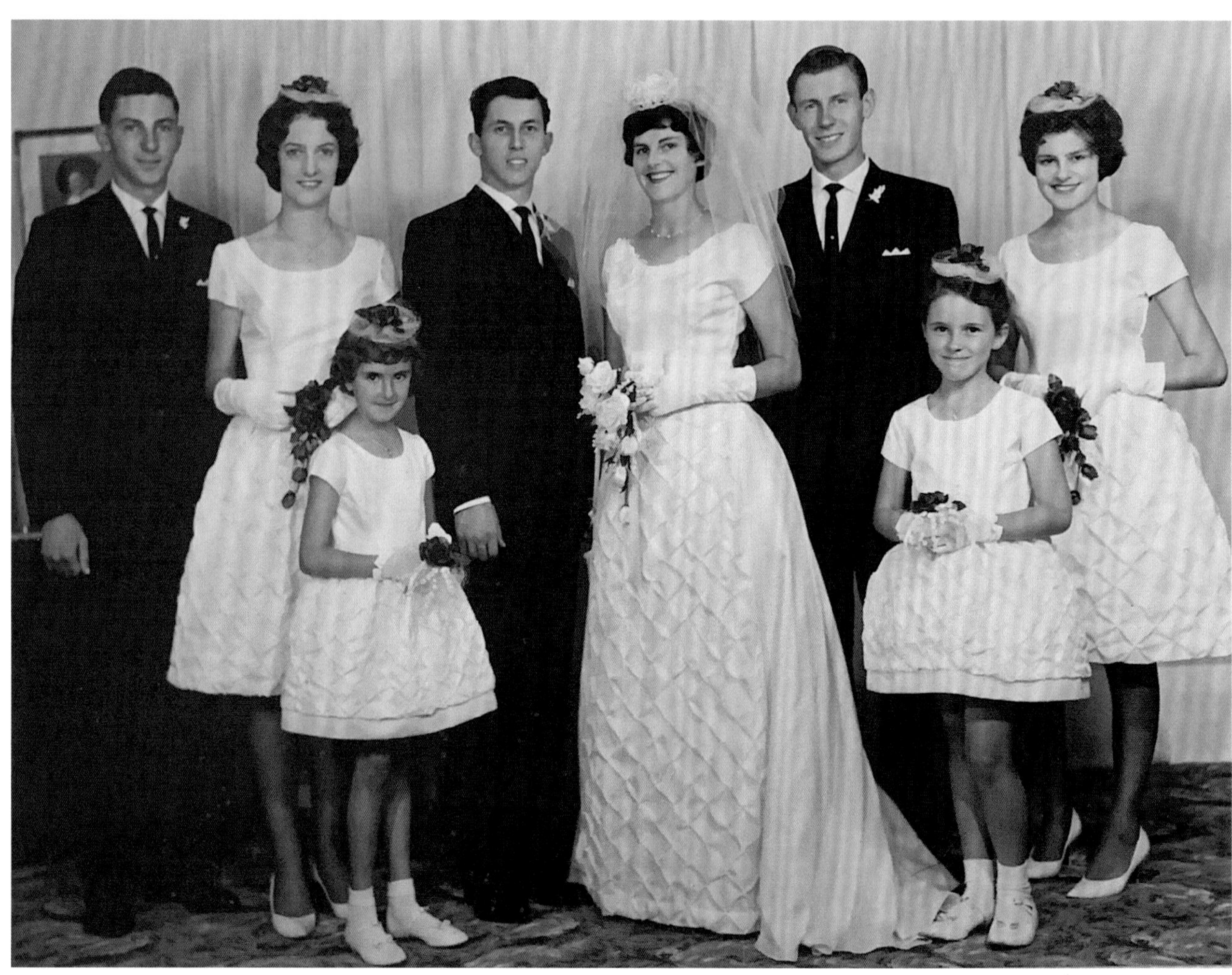

Above: Deane Hutton and Jan Thomson, 1963.

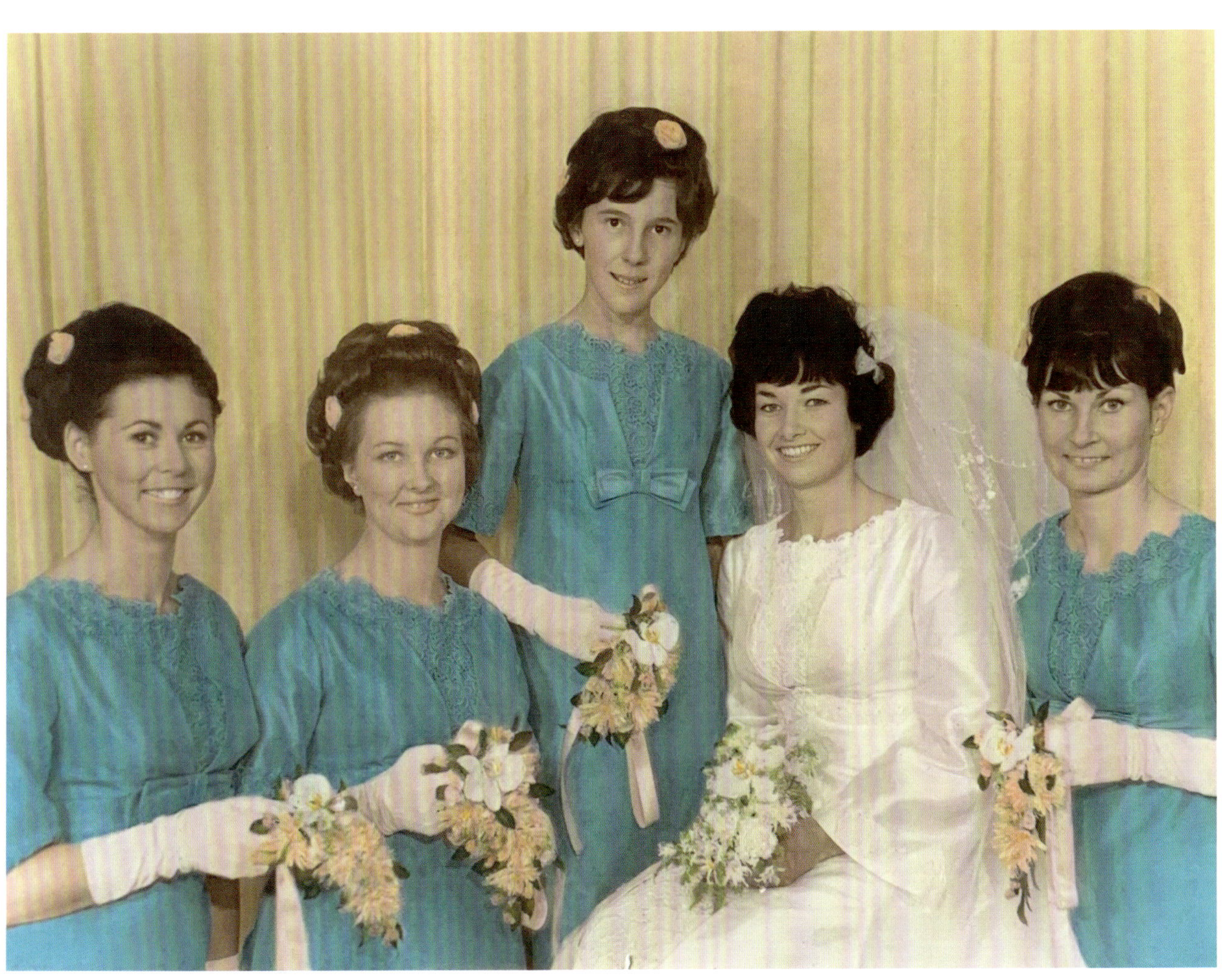

Above: Rex Hutton's bride Denny Stapledon, 1968.

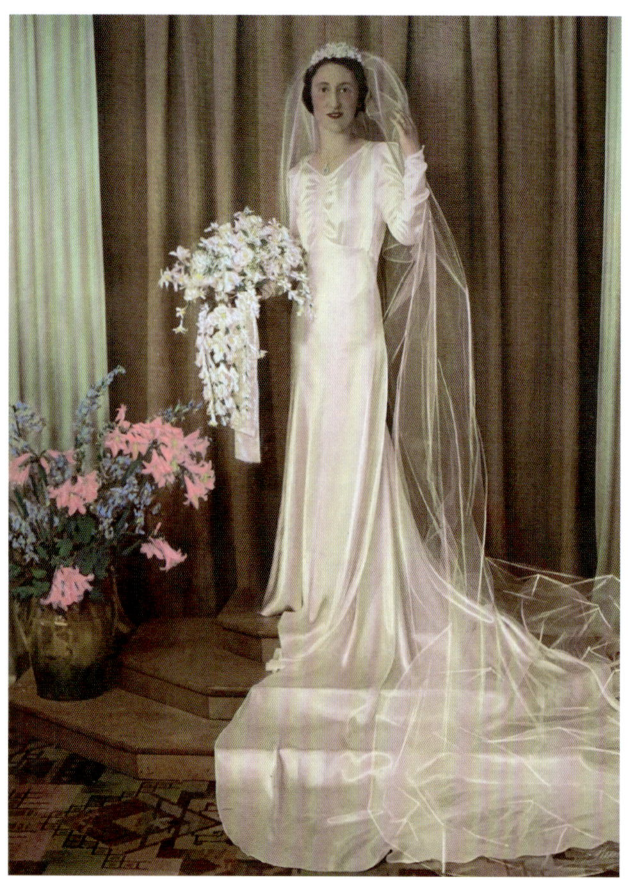

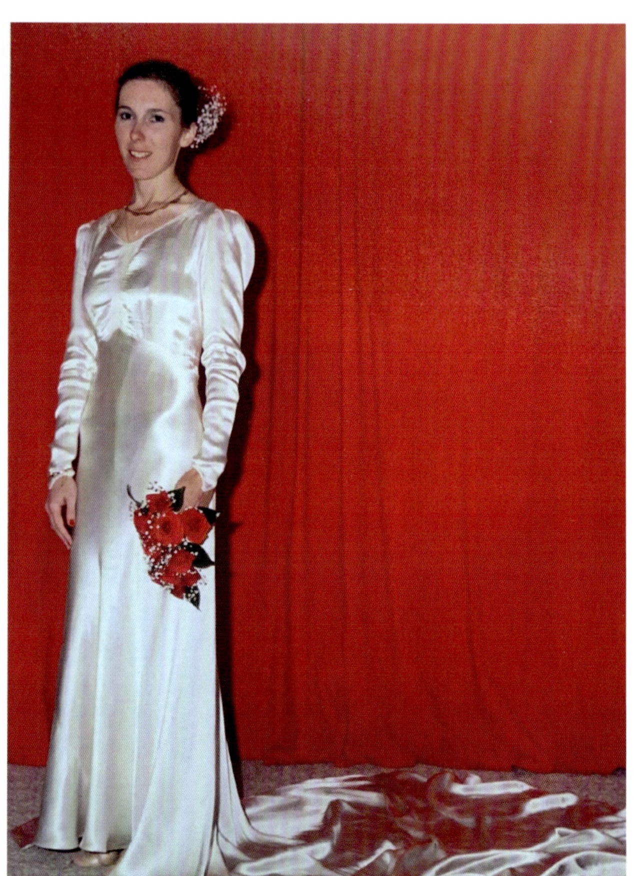

Above: Audrey Hutton, 1939.
Above right: Erina Newnham (née Hutton), 1980, wearing Audrey's 1939 dress.

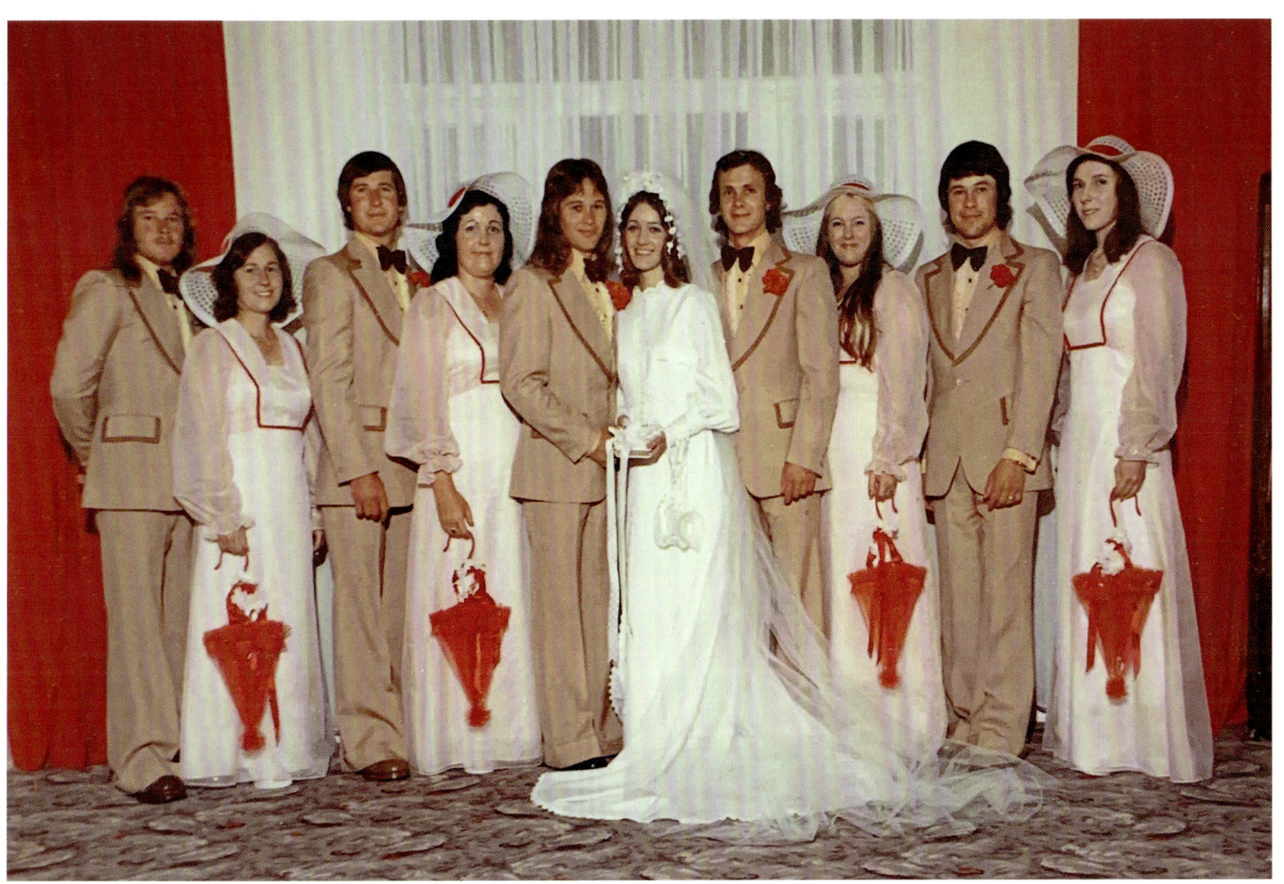

Above: Duke/Halls wedding, 1973.

The first photo in **1946** of sons Deane, Rex and Clive, which delighted the overseas photographer correspondents.

1954 A new baby arrived, after several years! A letter from friends interstate . . . 'we haven't recovered yet! The surprise of Christmas was your card . . . what a thrill for you to have a little daughter!'

1956 The Olympic Rings commemorated the games in Melbourne.

Biblical relevant references were sometimes added:

I Corinthians, ch 9 v 24–25 King James Version . . . *know ye not that they which run in a race run all, but one receiveth the prize? So run that ye may obtain. And every man that striveth for the mastery is temperate in all things. Now they do it to obtain a corruptible crown; but we are incorruptible.*

I John ch 5 v 4 KJV . . . *for whatsoever is born of God overcometh the world and this is the victory that overcometh the world: even our faith*

1960–61 A particularly challenging scene: various poses were taken and then cut out, the figures were then positioned on to an enlargement and rephotographed.

A friend and Baptist minister living in California observed . . . 'didn't know before, that one could get as much on a single record – ha. But of course see who does it!'

1963 Newlyweds Deane and Jan appeared on the newly acquired television.

1966 Youngest son Rex was away on National Service. The remaining Hutton offspring became Christmas tree baubles.

Luke Ch2, v 14 *Glory to God in the Highest, and on earth peace, goodwill to all men*

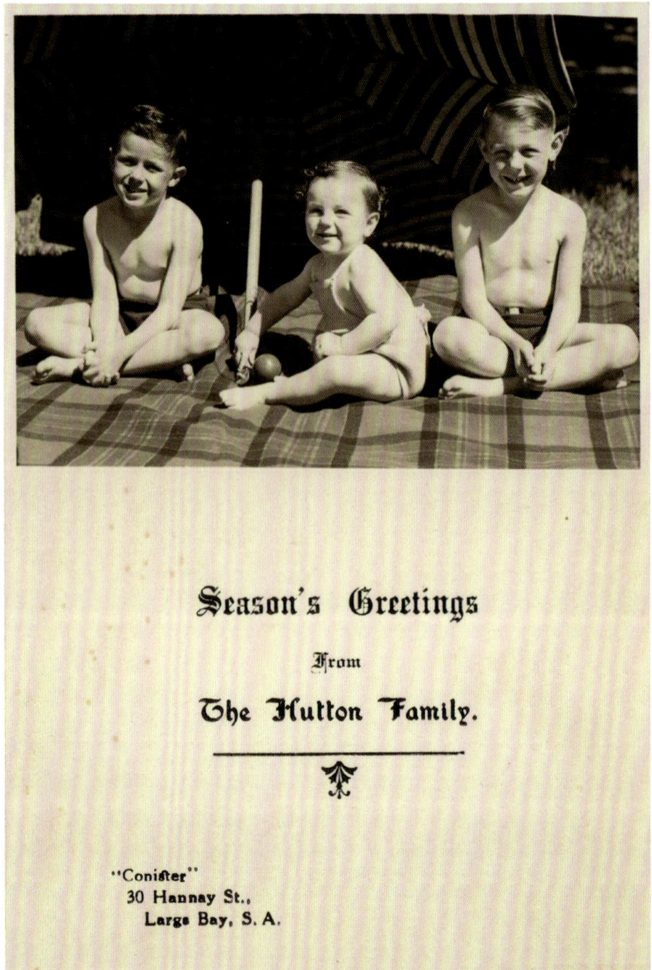

1968–69 Musical Christmas, Erina playing carols, Clive on newly acquired drums, Rex and Denny the newlyweds therein, George and Audrey appeared on TV, Deane was making his own cards with his young family.

1970 The last Christmas card of the expanding family, with three grandchildren and no gimmicks!

By **1975**, the four grandchildren posed in their Scottish outfits. By then the inspiration for new and different scenarios including the whole family had dwindled, and Audrey resorted to bought cards. Deane has continued the tradition with his expanding family for 53 years, since eldest son David was born.

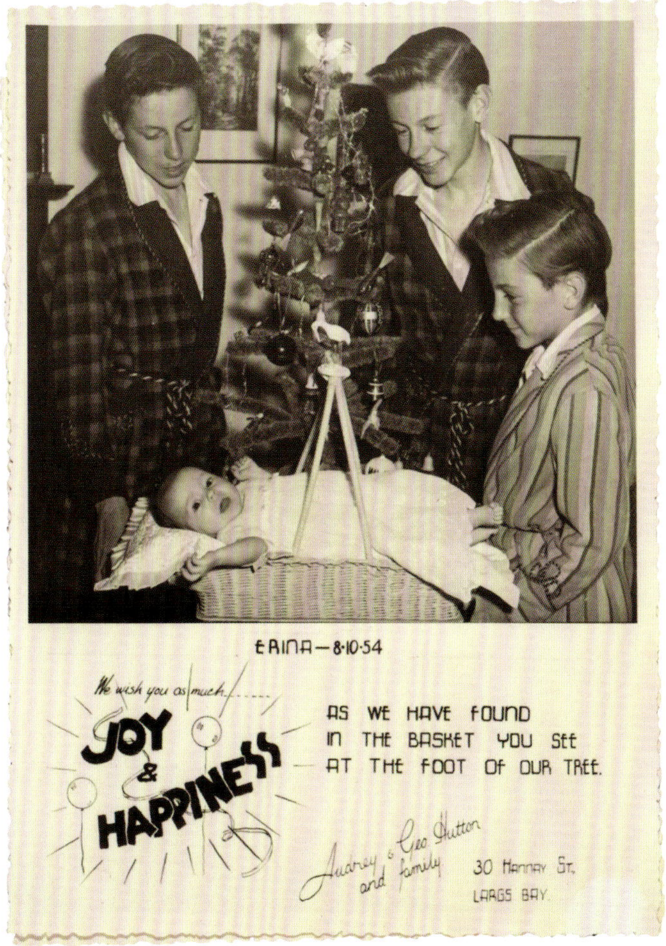
ERINA—8·10·54
We wish you as much
JOY & HAPPINESS
AS WE HAVE FOUND
IN THE BASKET YOU SEE
AT THE FOOT OF OUR TREE.
Audrey & Geo. Hutton and family
30 HANNAY ST.
LARGS BAY.

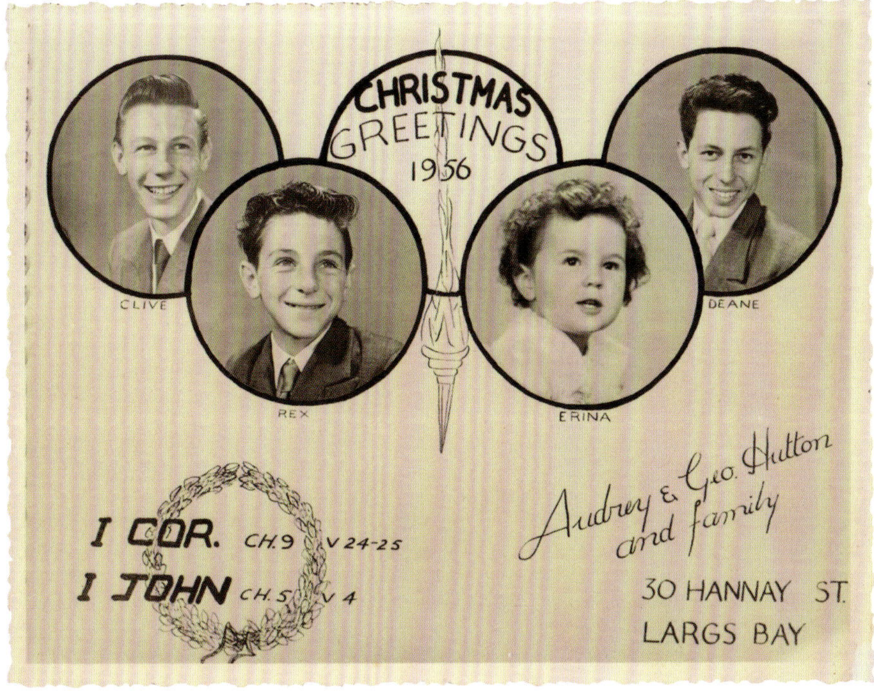
CHRISTMAS
GREETINGS
1956
CLIVE
REX
ERINA
DEANE
I COR. CH.9 V 24-25
I JOHN CH.5 V 4
Audrey & Geo. Hutton and family
30 HANNAY ST.
LARGS BAY

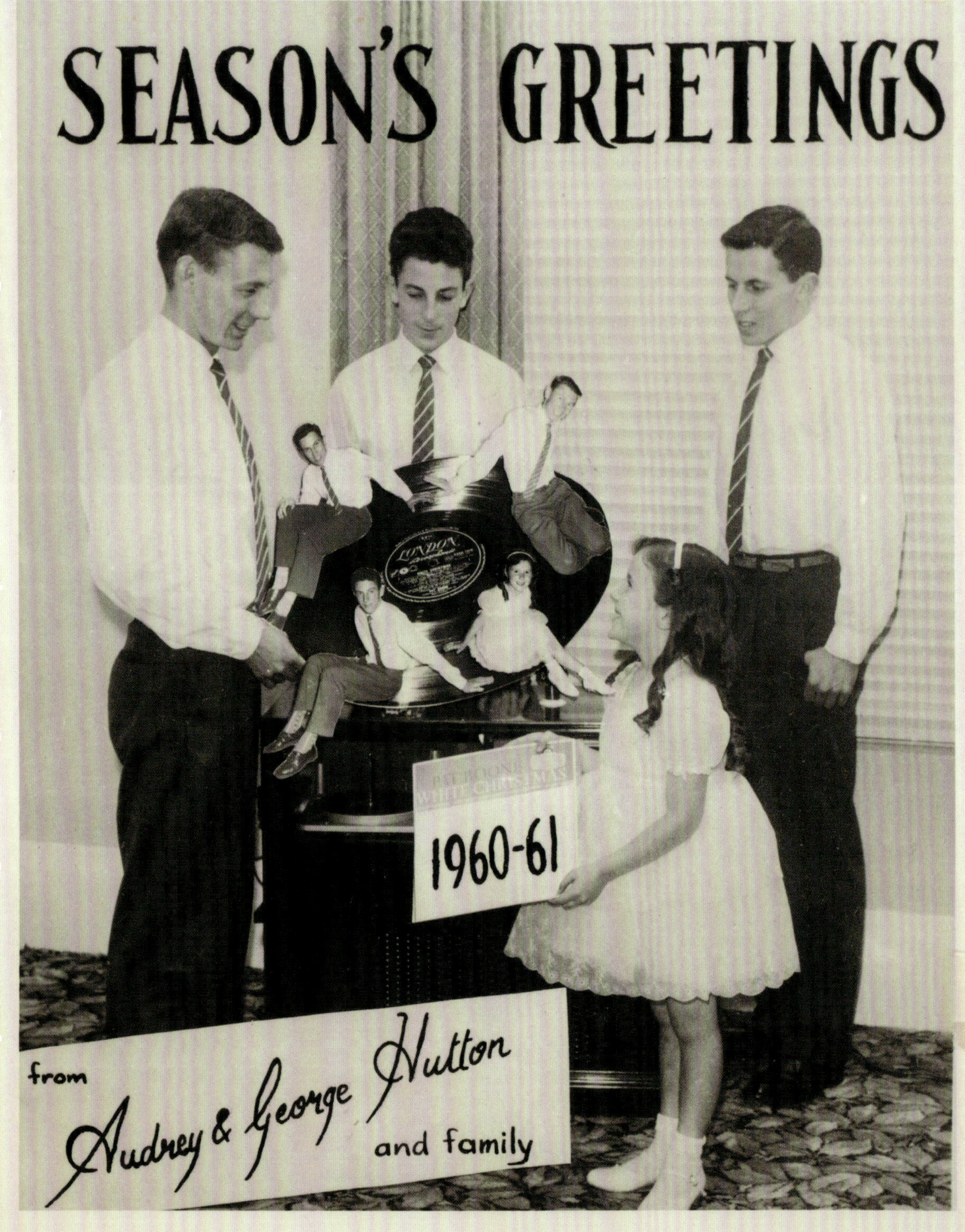
SEASON'S GREETINGS
1960-61
from
Audrey & George Hutton
and family

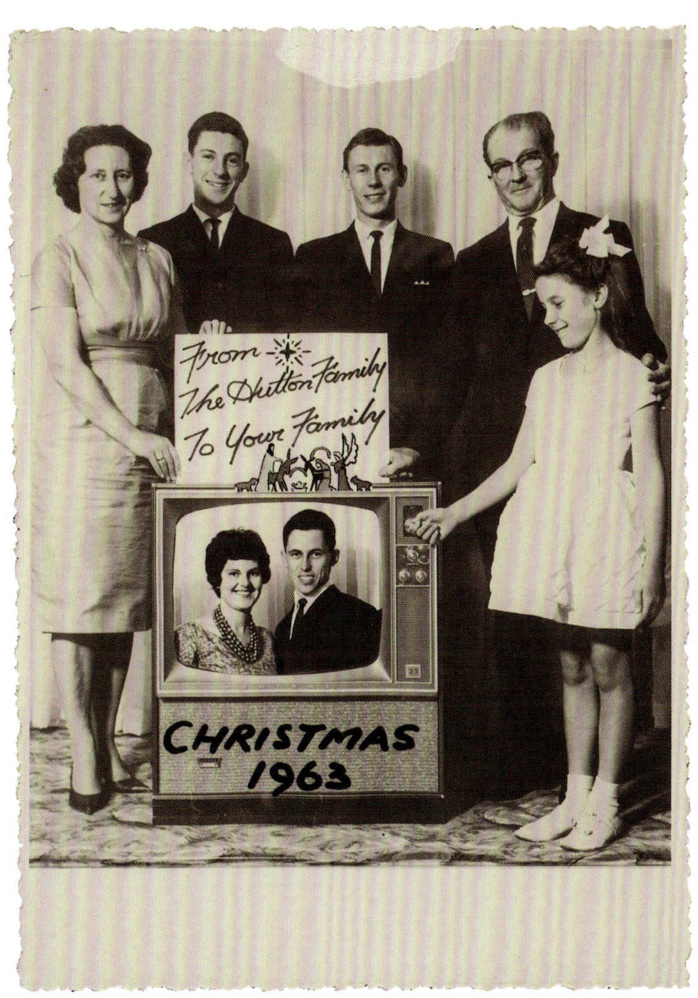
From
The Skilton Family
To Your Family
CHRISTMAS
1963

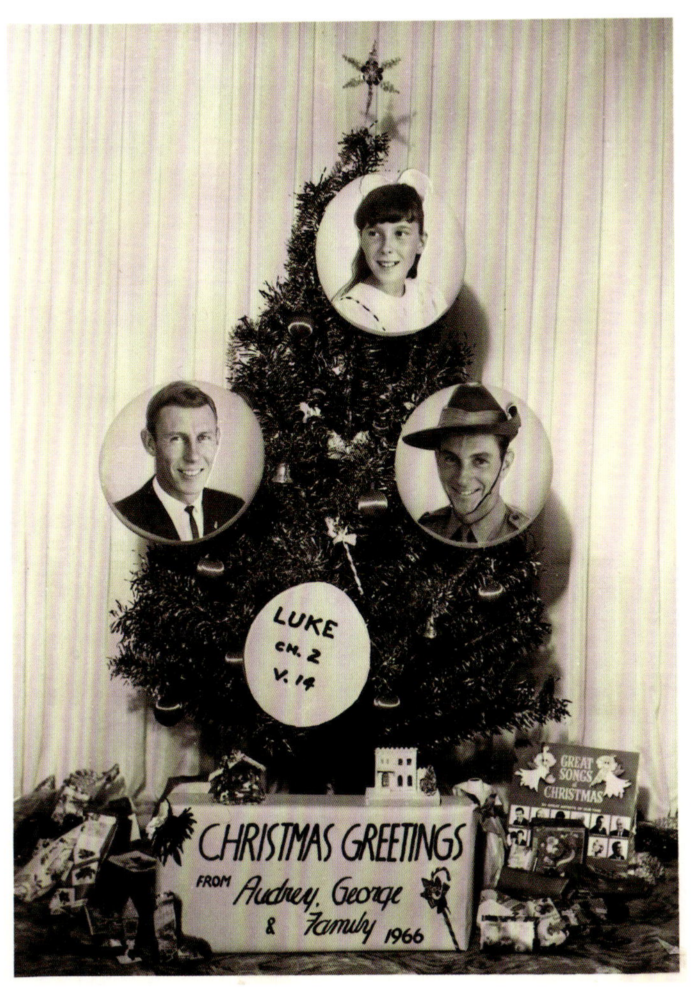
LUKE
CH. 2
V. 14
GREAT SONGS OF CHRISTMAS
CHRISTMAS GREETINGS
FROM Audrey, George
& Family 1966

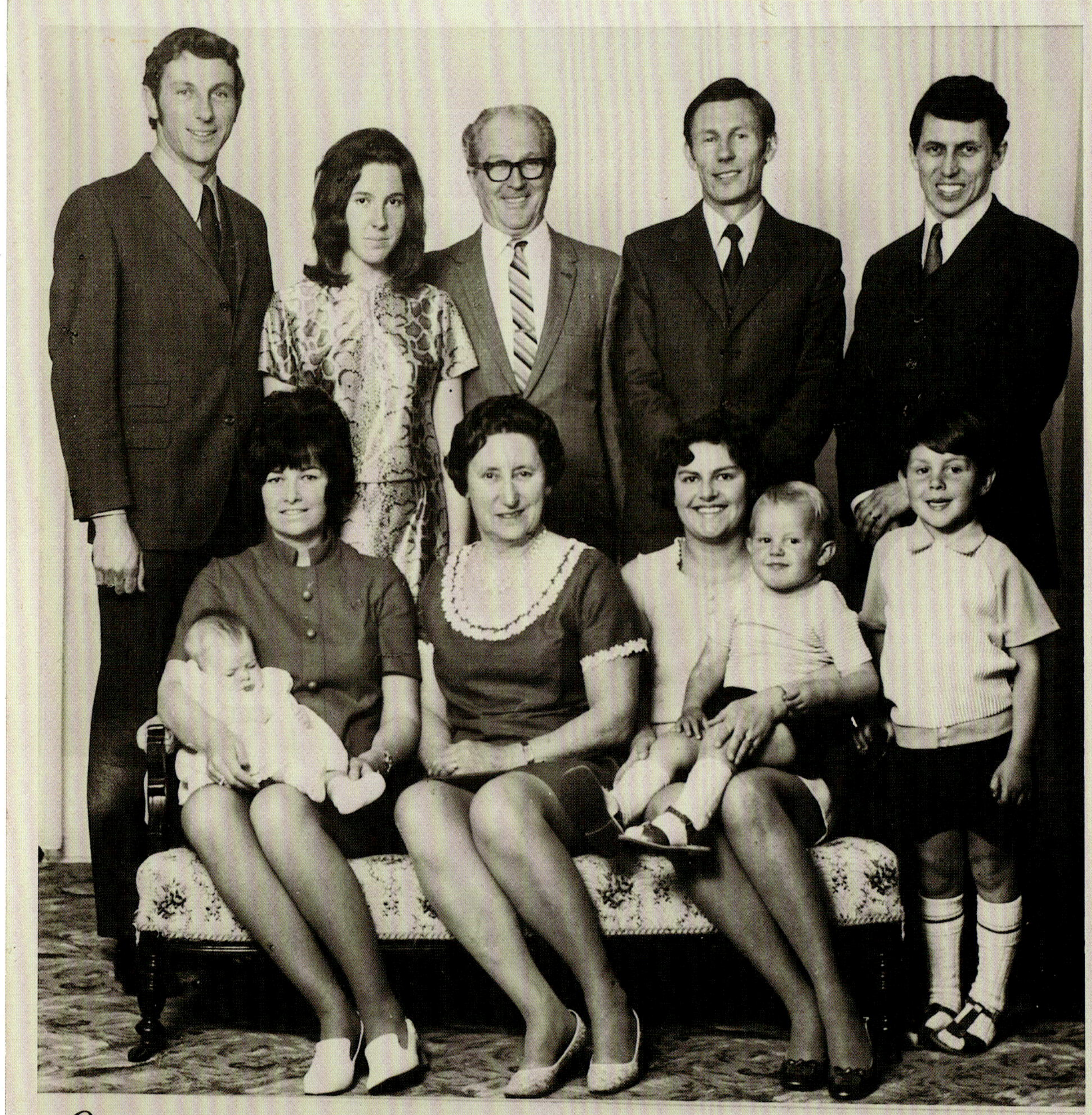

Greetings from

The Hutton Family

CHRISTMAS 1970

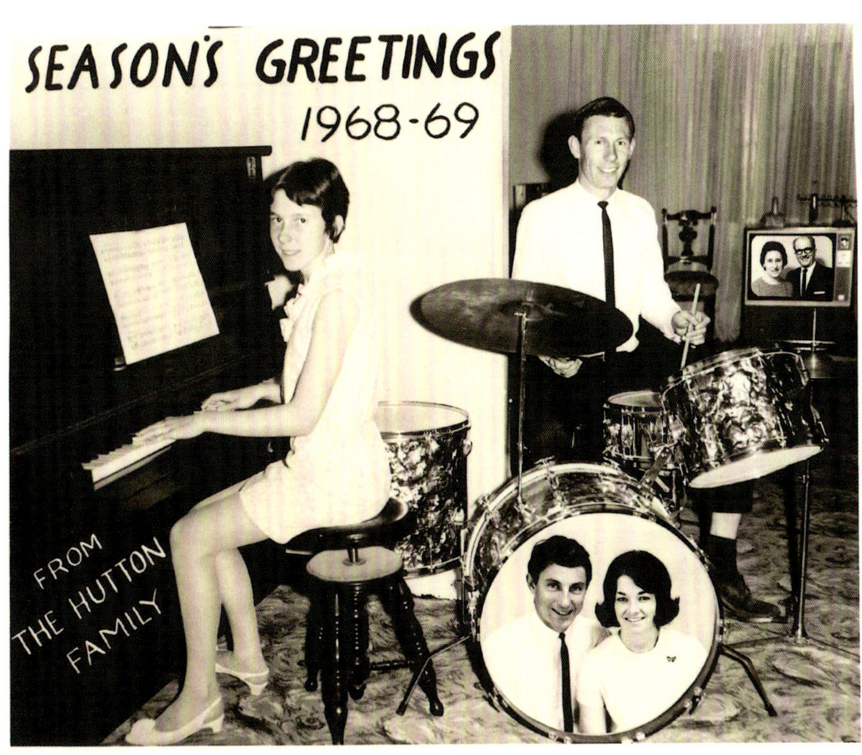
SEASON'S GREETINGS
1968-69
FROM
THE HUTTON
FAMILY

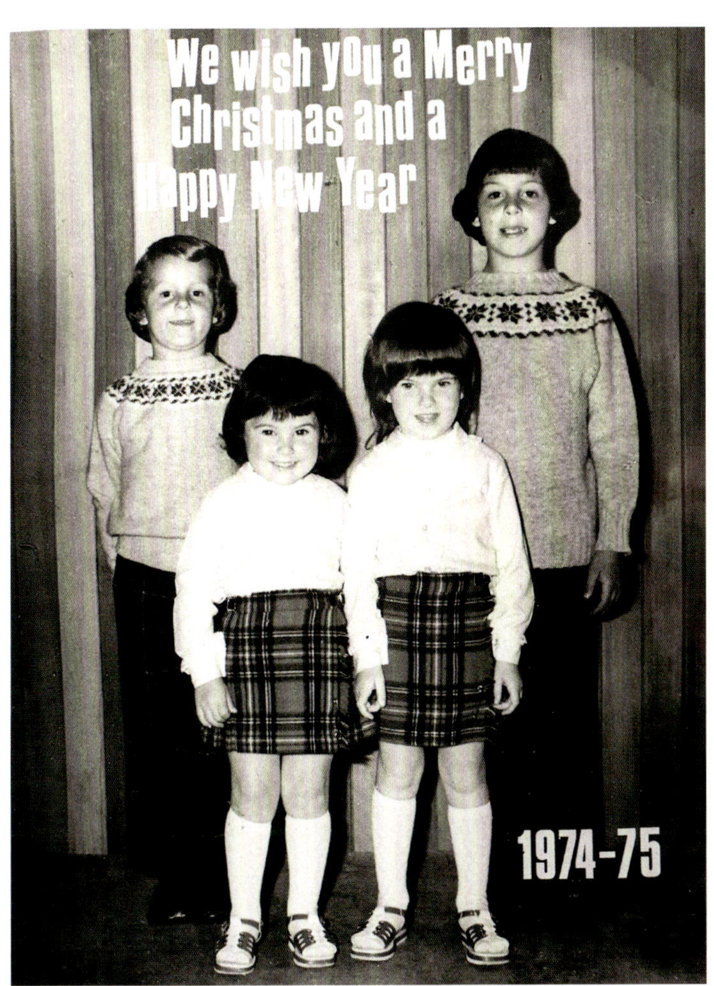
We wish you a Merry
Christmas and a
Happy New Year
1974-75

Wakefield Press is an independent publishing and
distribution company based in Adelaide, South Australia.
We love good stories and publish beautiful books.
To see our full range of books, please visit our website at
www.wakefieldpress.com.au
where all titles are available for purchase.
To keep up with our latest releases, news and events,
subscribe to our monthly newsletter.

Find us!

Facebook: www.facebook.com/wakefield.press
Twitter: www.twitter.com/wakefieldpress
Instagram: www.instagram.com/wakefieldpress